Broken Wings
of the Samurai

# Broken Wings
# of the Samurai

## The Destruction of the Japanese Airforce

## Robert C. Mikesh

**Naval Institute Press**
Annapolis, Maryland

Copyright © 1993 by Robert C. Mikesh

First published in the UK in 1993 by
Airlife Publishing Ltd.

Published and distributed in the United States of America and Canada by the
Naval Institute Press, US Naval Academy, 118 Maryland Avenue
Annapolis, Maryland 21402-5035

**Library of Congress Catalog Card Number**

ISBN 1-55750-083-5

Printed in England by Livesey Ltd., Shrewsbury.

# CONTENTS

# PREFACE

In August 1945, the greatest war of all times came to a conclusion. In leading to this climax, the substance of Japan had been gutted by mid-1945; the best of its army and navy had been defeated; the Japanese Homeland was at the mercy of air raids and inevitable invasion. In the tradition of *bushido*, some military leaders were dedicated to fight to the very end to defend their Emperor and country. In this endeavour, nearly 11,000 aircraft were available for kamikaze crash dives in this desperate effort to exert as much destruction against the invading forces as possible.

By the end of June 1945, 8,000 suicide or special-attack aircraft had been converted for this purpose from the 4,800 army and about 5,900 navy fighters, bombers, trainers, and reconnaissance aircraft that had survived the air battles. An additional 2,500 were expected to be converted for the kamikaze mission by late summer of that year.

The defensive attack plan was to conserve this air strength for employment against the landing forces. Carrier task forces supporting the invasion would be attacked by only a few hundred of these aircraft and then only when it became unmistakable that a full-scale invasion was in progress. The bulk of the remaining air fleet, mostly of the small special-attack type, would be launched against the warships and transports in the critical phase when boarding the assault barges in the invasion area. Japanese defenders expected to completely expend these aircraft within a ten-day period in a supreme effort to repel the invasion forces.

It was this strength of surviving aircraft that the occupying forces found when they arrived on Japanese soil. Of those thousands of aircraft, only a few remain today that stand as testimony to this once powerful air armada. These few survivors of the Imperial Japanese Air Forces are not generally looked upon today as instruments used to achieve Japanese aggression, but in the light of conventional air combat. They bring to mind the many air duals they fought by comparison with other warplanes of the opposing forces during the great Pacific War. More importantly, they serve as evidence of Japan's level to world standards in engineering technology by comparing them with aircraft of other nations for that time in world history. These relatively few surviving Japanese aircraft are all that remain as physical evidence of this once powerful and mighty air strength. Because of this, it is appropriate that the first chapter of this book describes this strength, how it was achieved, and finally exhausted at the time of Japan's surrender.

Like the **Samurai** of earlier years, these Japanese fighter pilots were dedicated to fight for their country and their Emperor to the very end if needed. *(S Hayashi)*

After the period of extended deadly conflict, it was only natural that tools of war would be objects quickly placed aside and disposed of in most cases. This was accomplished at a rapid pace following World War II. Much of Japan's best technology of that period was destroyed in the process. For that which survived to the end of that war and beyond, this book holds that concluding chapter. Such an undertaking cannot be the work of one person, but instead, the assistance of many, bringing together knowledge and specialization from many quarters.

This book would have never been conceived had it not been for the suggestion of this author's long time friend, James P Gallagher. He proposed that I freely use any and all of his classic photographs in a book of my choice that were contained in his earlier book *Meatballs and Dead Birds*. Now, with these photographs available for a second time, historians and hobbyists that missed these pictures in their first showing, have access to this valued material. For this opportunity and confidence offered by Jim Gallagher, I am most grateful.

The gathering of other photographs* was particularly important to this coverage. There are far too many who have contributed to mention here, yet my thanks go to all who have been so willing to make their photographs available. Major contributors include Shigeo Hayashi with his first generation of magnificent war-time action photographs, many of which were printed exclusively for this book. Thanks also to Richard L Seely for making his, and the extensive R M Bueschel photos now in his collection available to me, John and Donna Campbell, of the Campbell Aviation Photography Archives for many of these prints, and Mark Clayton with "down under" photographs otherwise difficult to obtain.

There are many technical aspects of this book that may not be readily apparent to the casual reader. In order to assure accuracy in events, locations, and many other historical aspects contained in this book, the author relied upon the assistance of many for their specialities. Among those in the United States in alphabetical order are; David Aiken, Richard M Bueschel, James F Lansdale, James I Long, Al Makiel, Edward T Maloney, David W Menard, George Poling, and Steve Remington. Contributors from other parts of the world added their knowledge in compiling this material. In Australia, my appreciation goes to Mark Clayton and William L Holswich for their help from that part of the world. In England, Bob Ogden was very supportive with material gained from his publication covering **Aircraft Museums and Collections of the World, 1: Asia** edition. Naturally I relied heavily on Japanese support for some of this coverage. Among those to whom I send my thanks are: Shorzoe Abe, Nobuo Harada, Osamu "Sam" and Yoshio Tagaya. In the interest of space, other names must be omitted, but this author recognizes very fully the important contribution the named and the unnamed have made to this publication.

*Photograph credit prefix 80-G indicates photographs sourced from the US Navy Collection, National Archive, Washington DC.

Photograph credit prefix SC indicates photographs sourced from the US Army Collection, National Archive, Washington DC.

Photograph credit suffix AC indicates photographs sourced from the US Air Force Collection, National Air & Space Museum, Washington DC.

Photograph credit prefix USMC indicates photographs sourced from the US Marine Corps Collection, National Archive, Washington DC.

Photograph credit prefix NASM indicates photographs sourced from National Air & Space Museum, Smithsonian Institution, Washington DC.

# CHAPTER I
# THE WAR YEARS

## From Strength to Defeat

The capability of the Mitsubishi Navy G3M1 Attack Bombers surprised the world when they became the first bombers to conduct an international strike when attacking China from the main islands of Japan in August 1937. They were later code named "Nell" by the Allied Forces.

When Japan launched its opening attack of the Pacific War on 7 December , 1941, it was master of the largest military force in the Pacific. The war that ensued did not become a sea, ground, or air war, but a combination of all three in a three dimensional conflict. Air superiority was essential in the success of all these elements and Japan was confident that it had this capability because of a well calculated strength build-up over the preceding years. Japan was not prepared for a prolonged war which became an afterthought by its leaders following initial successes. As the war persisted, Allied strength continued to build while Japan's ability to replenish its losses became overwhelmed. With this came the loss of air superiority for Japan, and thus, the eventual defeat of that nation.

When the war erupted in the Pacific, it was as though the Zero Fighter was in every part of the Pacific overnight. In the early months they were thought to be invincible.

Japan had the upper hand in the opening stages of the war by determining where and when the air battles would take place. Shown here are Zero Model 22s of the First *Kokutai* (Naval Air Group) in Rabaul engaging in Operation *Ro-Go*, November 2-12, 1943.

The cause that brought about Japan's need to build its forces in the Pacific can be traced to the Washington Conference and the Naval Armaments Treaty that evolved and was agreed to in 1922. Its purpose was to prevent Japan causing an imbalance in major warship tonnage to that of the navies of the United States and Great Britain. However, the latter two nations had to divide their navies over two oceans, while still blanketing the entire Pacific Ocean to protect its possessions, resources and supply routes. Japan, on the other hand, had a far less area to cover and defend, an area much closer to its homeland than the other two nations. Should Japan plan an aggressive attack, her forces could be consolidated for that attack while the defenders had to be on the alert over the entire Pacific Ocean area. This was the case when Japan attacked Pearl Harbor.

The issue that gave Japan the advantage was its superior strength in air power. While combined tonnage of the major naval fleets of the world was controlled by international agreements, the quantity and types of aircraft to support these fleets were never a factor, although once considered. Japan recognized the potential of air power, and in the 1930s began a major build-up to capitalize upon this strength.

The Mitsubishi Navy G4M1 Attack Bomber "Betty" was a land-based bomber designed to support Japanese fleet activities at great range and therefore not be dependent upon the fleet for its own support.

## The War Years

As the war began between Japan and the Allied forces in the Pacific, Japan had in readiness 2,700 aircraft[1] in fully-trained and organized air units. For the Allied forces scattered in other parts of the Pacific, at Midway, Wake Island, the Philippines, Netherlands East Indies, and Hawaii, their total aircraft count was 1,426, of which only 688 were considered first-line equipment. Within this number, the British and Australians possessed 332 aircraft[2]. RAF pilots had combat experience, and were probably as good as the Japanese, but their aircraft were old or no match for Japanese aircraft.

The war, in terms of Japanese air operations, can be viewed in three distinct phases. The first phase is that of Japanese advances when the Japanese Air Forces gained superiority in every theatre in preparation for ground and amphibious operations. The second phase was the time the Japanese Air Forces lost air superiority in these theatres and the Allies began to advance, exploiting their own air superiority. The final phase was when the Japanese turned their attention to the creation of special suicide attack forces designed to turn back an invasion of the main Japanese Islands.

When the Japanese had the advantage during the first four months of the war, their air forces gained and maintained air superiority over the Philippines, the Netherlands East Indies, and South-east Asia as Japanese ground and amphibious forces swept forward. In a single week, the Japanese Navy carried out the Pearl Harbor attack, putting eight battleships out of action and crippling United States air power in the Pacific; it sunk the British warships *Repulse* and *Prince of Wales;* and it nearly completed the destruction of the numerically small and in part obsolete United States Army Air Force in the Philippines. The Japanese Army Air Force was not so spectacular, but it played the major part in achieving air superiority in South-east Asia, and assisted the Japanese Navy in the Philippines.

The air groups employed in the Pearl Harbor operations were the finest in the Japanese Air Forces. Each was well trained even in 1940, and they were reinforced for this occasion with specially picked pilots from almost every group in Japan. Special training was begun in August 1941 with the problems of the particular operation in view. Emphasis was placed on shallow water torpedo attacks in waters no deeper than Pearl Harbor, and special horizontal and dive bombing tactics were practised as well. When the groups embarked in November, they were among the most dangerous units ever assembled by any air force to that time. The attack did not go without cost to the Japanese however. Of the 414 aircraft assigned to the six aircraft carriers, twenty-nine aircraft did not return. This was a small loss considering what military planners were braced to accept, and compared to the hundreds of aircraft losses in air battles that lay ahead.

The Japanese attack upon Wake Island on 8 and 9 December was carried out by the Japanese Navy air group stationed in the Marshalls, well trained in over-water navigation and support of fleet operations. But the first Japanese attempt to land on Wake was beaten off on 10 December and, accordingly, on 22 December two of the Pearl Harbor carriers were brought in to carry out additional strikes. These aircraft wiped out the remaining American Grumman F4F Wildcat fighters and assisted

Designed for carrier operations with the Japanese fleet, the Mitsubishi Zero Fighters served equally as well when operating from land bases throughout the Pacific.

Considered to have been the best performing 4-engine flying-boat of the Pacific War was this Kawanishi Navy H8K2 Flying-boat, Allied code named "Emily". They not only carried a heavy load but had exceptional long range and high speed for their size.

---

1: Japanese Air Power, US Strategic Bombing Survey. p.4.

2: Trevor Nevitt Dupuy *Military History of World War II: Vol 13*, (Franklin Watts, New York, 1964, p.14.

materially in the success of the landing on 23 December. The occupation of other islands by Japanese forces, such as Guam, soon followed.

When Japanese attention was turned towards the occupation of the Philippines, the primary mission of both Japanese Army and Navy Air Forces was the destruction of the United States air power. First estimates by the Japanese of US strength amounted to 300 first-line aircraft based upon aerial photographs. Actually there were only about 160 combat aircraft, including twenty-nine obsolete aircraft of the Philippines Air Force. The Japanese knew they would have numerical and qualitative superiority, and they proceeded accordingly.

The destruction of American air power in the Philippines was accomplished by repeated attacks on Clark Field and air bases around Manila. The Japanese Army quickly established airfields in occupied portions of the Philippines in order to provide close support for the main Japanese thrust south from Lingayen Gulf towards Manila. The defending forces were generally removed to southern bases in order to conserve what little strength remained for reconnaissance missions.

Manila fell into the hands of the advancing army on 2 January, 1942. It was a matter of time before all of the Philippines would be in the hands of the Japanese. By a combination of superior skill and organization, weight of numbers, surprise and good fortune, Japan had won the first air battle of the Philippines.

Scouting duties for the fleet were shared by Nakajima Navy E8N2 Reconnaissance Seaplanes, code named "Dave". These floatplanes were catapult-launched from battleships and cruisers of the Japanese fleet, and remained operational well into the war years.

The Mitsubishi Army Ki-21 Heavy Bomber was first line equipment at the beginning of the Pacific War. Known as "Sally", they contributed more than any other aircraft to bringing the air branch of the Japanese Army to world standards when first placed into service. *(USAF 26514 AC)*

Fighting a war over the Pacific, the Japanese Navy used seaplane fighters based at the many island bases that were without shore-based runways. Shown here are float-equipped Zeros Fighters, code named "Rufe".

The Zero Fighter was a highly manoeuvrable aircraft mainly because of its lightweight construction. It was superior against the US Navy's Wildcat, but not the later Hellcat which was more rugged and had greater engine performance and firepower.

The Kawanishi Navy H6K5 flying-boat "Mavis" was heavily relied upon by the Japanese to connect the far reaches of the Pacific. Obsolete at the time the Pacific War began, they served well into the mid part of that war.

The standard fighter for the Japanese Army was the Nakajima Army Ki-43-II Hayabusa and code named "Oscar". Thought by some as an "Army Zero", it was an entirely different design of the same time period, with the same type engine.

As Japan's southern advance into the Netherlands East Indies began, Allied air opposition was all but negligible. The Allied air attack warning system was very poor, and the Japanese time and again caught Allied aircraft on the ground and destroyed them. Moreover, the Japanese enjoyed a numerical superiority of at least four to one at every point they chose to attack. Their pilots for the most part were more experienced than the Allied pilots, most of them having had no previous combat experience.

By 19 February, Australia was severely threatened when aircraft from Japanese aircraft carriers attacked Darwin, the Australian terminus of the 1,300 mile ferry route from Java to the west. The force overwhelmed the ten intercepting American fighters, destroyed almost all important air installations, warehouses and docks and sank virtually every vessel in Port Darwin harbour. About a week later, Japanese land-based bombers sank the USS *Langley*, which was attempting to ferry Curtiss P-40s from Australia to Java. Because of the superiority of Japanese air power, the Allied air operations in the Netherlands East Indies came abruptly to a halt.

Meanwhile, the Japanese had also penetrated into New Guinea and the Bismarks, landing at Rabaul on 22 January and making their first air raid on Port Moresby ten days later. In this area the Japanese enjoyed air superiority from the beginning, for the Australians possessed only twenty Lockheed Hudson bombers, fourteen Catalina flying-boats, and no fighters to oppose the Japanese, only a handful of Wirraway lightly-armed advanced trainers to counter 100 attacking Japanese aircraft.

A sturdy bomber of the Japanese Army was this Mitsubishi Ki-67 Hiryu. It appeared late in the war in October 1944 and in addition to level bombing, it was noted for its torpedo attacks. Known as "Peggy", it is one of the few types to serve both the Army and the Navy.

The Mitsubishi Ki-46 "Dinah" was an exceptional aircraft in speed and mission capability. This was an Army reconnaissance aircraft that gave any Allied fighter a difficult interception problem.

(S Hayashi)

The Army's Nakajima Ki-43-II "Oscar 2" was a nimble fighter which made its mark wherever it fought in support of the Army. Like the Zero, it too was initially without armour or fuel tank protection, but in turn, this did enhance its fighting manoeuvrability.

Japanese advances were not solely attributed to overwhelming strength in numbers. Its aircraft was superior in many ways. The Zero fighter, first fully appreciated over Pearl Harbor, was looked upon as nearly invincible because of its speed and manoeuvrability. Other Japanese fighters encountered by Allied pilots were treated with respect. Its bombers were fast and carried heavy loads that disrupted Allied re-supply lines and marshalling yards. As long as they could have adequate fighter protection, they handled these missions very well. Japan had reached, and in many cases, exceeded aviation technology to that of the western powers for that time of the war.

As the Japanese penetrated deeply into the Malayan Peninsula, these operations ranked with those of the later battles over the Solomons, the second Philippines and the Okinawa campaigns as the largest and most sustained air operations ever conducted by the Japanese Air Forces. The attacks on Singapore in preparation for the ground assault were very large and sustained by Japanese standards, though small in comparison with Allied air operations in the European theatre or later against Japan. They involved some 4,000 sorties in the course of which 1,500 tons of bombs were dropped. The primary targets were RAF airfields. The British naval base was deliberately left untouched for future use by the Japanese.

Two of the "heavies" in the Japanese bomber force are these Nakajima Ki-49 Donryu, known to the Allies as "Helen". Small in number at the beginning of the war, production increased whereby their effectiveness was felt throughout the war. *(S Hayashi)*

Kawasaki Ki-45-Kai-C "Nick" two-seat fighters of the 3rd Chutai, 53rd Fighter Sentai operated from Kashiwa Air Base north-east of Tokyo. Note the twin 20 mm cannon behind the cockpit that fired upward at a 30 degree angle. This method of attack was very lethal when interdicting B-29s at night. *(S Hayashi)*

## Turn of Events

Four months after the war began, mid-April 1942, the Japanese Air Forces had not suffered a single serious reverse. In every theatre they enjoyed apparent air superiority to the point that on 9 and 12 April their carriers were able to strike at Ceylon, 7,000 miles from the main islands of Japan, and the furthest point from Japan hit by Japanese forces other than submarines.

The shock created by the Doolittle raid upon the heartland of Japan on 18 April 1942 by B-25s from the United States Navy carrier USS *Hornet* suddenly caused the Japanese to consider the defence of the home islands, a consideration that had received scant attention. Two new Army fighter groups were organized and based in Japan, and three more were converted from a training to a defence status. A total of four Army fighter groups were held in Japan throughout 1942 and 1943 for the defence of the homeland at a time when the Japanese Navy was urgently demanding that the Army send reinforcements to the Solomons.

An additional move on the part of the Japanese to counter any further intrusions by American aircraft carrier strikes upon their homeland was their plan to extend their perimeter of control. They decided to seize Midway Island and establish bases in the Aleutian Islands. In addition, they moved to the south-east by seizing Port Moresby in southern New Guinea, and by establishing air and naval bases in the southern Solomon Islands. From this resulted the Battle of the Coral Sea (4–8 May 1942) always to be noted as the first important victory for Allied air power in the Far East and the turning of the war in disfavour of Japan. That action involved Japanese amphibious forces that were attempting to take Port Moresby. The US Navy engaged the Japanese forces at sea, not by surface craft, but instead, this became the first important engagement in naval history decided entirely by air operations.

One month later when the Japanese made their attempt at Midway, Japan lost four of her six regular carriers, a cruiser and 250 aircraft, while US losses were the carrier USS *Yorktown,* a destroyer and 150 aircraft. The Japanese carrier force never recovered and could never again be used as an offensive weapon.

Guadalcanal was another one of these major turning points of the war. In August 1942 the United States marines landed on that island. This was followed by a series of air battles in which the Japanese Navy lost a very large proportion of the pilots. Many of these losses were seasoned pilots having experience from the start of this war. During 1943 and early 1944, the Army air arm lost almost as heavily in New Guinea, in part because it could not muster the supply, maintenance and medical problems incident to operations in a tropical climate far from main depots. With its supply lines virtually cut by Allied submarines, it was now apparent that Japan had extended its operations far beyond the distances that it could logistically support.

In Burma and China, the Japanese high command had given these air operations a low priority. The result was that in those theatres the Allies had won air superiority in 1944 almost by default.

Engagement after engagement followed, all with expected high losses for both sides. The Allies had developed a supply and training system of replacements, while the Japanese remained very limited in this respect. It was by now very apparent that Japan was in retreat because of loss of air superiority. Her supply lines to distant fighting locations were frequently severed, either by Allied submarines or air interception. Japanese combat aircraft were frequently stranded on the ground for want of one, yet vital, part. Operational aircraft often became victims of parts cannibalization in order to keep others in the air. This was an expensive and impractical means of parts re-supply. It was not uncommon for advancing Allied forces, when reaching these captured Japanese airfields, to find undamaged aircraft, stripped of usable parts to repair other aircraft.

Japan was not prepared for a lengthy war, one that called for the rapid re-supply of attrition. The capability of mass production as known in the United States was never achieved. Factories were eventually the targets of American bombers. Cottage industries were a major supplier of aircraft parts, and to change production to newer aircraft was extremely difficult.

As an example, the Mitsubishi Zero, the most staunch fighter aircraft of the Japanese Navy in the early stages of the war, remained in combat to the very end, even though outclassed by Allied fighters as well as those of other Japanese designs. Production of any type was greatly inhibited because of the production methods used. The Air Ministry recognized the loss in fighter production numbers should a total conversion be expected for new designs. In order to sustain production quantities, the Zero was continued to the end of the war, and only controlled aspects of factory production were devoted to the newer designs which in themselves were frequently interrupted by air attacks, parts and material shortages.

The lack of trained pilots was another cause for heavy losses of aircraft. As Allied air engagements overpowered the trained corps of Japanese pilots, the quantity of replacements were not in the training phases to the degree needed. Once this was recognized and new recruits inducted for pilot training, they had to be pressed into combat units before becoming fully competent with their aircraft. This in itself placed them at a disadvantage against the better trained Allied pilots which resulted in heavy losses to the Japanese.

Armourers prepare this Kawasaki Ki-45 kai for an interception mission from Kashiwa Air Base. They are loading the forward firing 37 mm nose cannon. In the belly tunnel is a similar cannon for frontal attacks. This was a hard-hitting fighter against ground targets for the Japanese Army. (S Hayashi)

This rare photograph shows three Kawasaki Ki-45-Kai "Nick" two-seat fighters of the 3rd Chutai, 53rd Fighter Sentai flying in the Tokyo area. These aircraft are equipped for the night fighter intercept mission, having two 20 mm cannon fixed to fire upward behind the pilot's cockpit. (S Hayashi)

Losses of aircraft in ferrying were heavy because of lack of training in navigation; one unit alone lost eighteen aircraft, half its strength, on a flight between Truk and Rabaul. Again, the extended logistic supply lines exceeded Japan's capability. Because of the inexperience of the ferry pilots, bad maintenance along the route, and the poor condition of the forward fields, many aircraft were unfit for combat when they reached their forward areas, thus becoming non-combat losses.

In nearly every campaign that followed, the Japanese sustained very heavy air losses. The Battle of the Philippine Sea is but one of these times of heavy losses for the Japanese. A newly-formed task force of the Japanese Fleet was to inflict a damaging blow to the US Seventh Fleet which was engaged in the support of landing operations on Saipan and Tinian in the Marianas in June 1944. Beginning at 10:00 hours on the morning of 19 June, 1944, the Japanese carrier aircraft began their attacks against the American fleet. But either because of tactical error or poor state of training of the Japanese pilots, the attacks came in widely separated waves and with little co-ordination between waves.

US Navy F6F Hellcats were waiting high above the fleet. Only about forty of the Japanese aircraft got past these defensive fighters, and half of those remaining were shot down by the ships' curtain of intensive anti-aircraft fire. Bomb hits caused slight damage to the US ships, and no American warships suffered any loss in fighting efficiency.

About 370 Japanese aircraft were shot down during this spectacular aerial battle, which the American flyers called the "Marianas Turkey Shoot". Counting the land-based aircraft destroyed in the early morning, total Japanese losses were more than 400 aircraft. Twenty-six American aircraft were lost; but about half of their pilots were saved. For the month of June alone, Japanese losses amounted to about 1,000 aircraft.

Pilot training for both services was slow in providing well-trained pilots to replace losses as the war accelerated. By the end of the war, the 18,000 Japanese pilots available for combat had a low average flying experience of about 100 hours.

Coming to life with an external starter is this 350 hp Hitachi engine that powers the Army's Tachikawa Ki-9 "Spruce" intermediate training aircraft. The tail insignia identifies the Army Officers Training School at Irumagawa Air Base near Tokyo.

In another engagement brought about as US carriers swept the Ryukyus, Formosa, and Luzon in a series of strikes designed to screen the Leyte landings, Japanese Navy Air Force units in Kyushu were brought into action. On 12 October 1944, the Japanese sortied in night torpedo attacks against the US carriers as well as dive-bombing attacks. The returning pilots reported sinking five major fleet units, and thereafter, all caution was abandoned and all available aircraft were sent out in an attempt to sink the remains of the US Fleet. In all, some 700 sorties were flown against the Task Force, and the Japanese public was told that there had been a resounding victory with 30 Allied ships sunk.

Actually, no ships were sunk and only two cruisers were damaged, while the Japanese lost at least 400 aircraft and pilots. Although very inexperienced by Allied standards, the pilots probably were the best remaining in the Japanese Navy Air Force, and their loss reduced the quality of the Navy Air Force even further.

Used in greater numbers than any other Japanese Army intercepter was the Nakajima Ki-44 Shoki. They first appeared in China in 1942, moving to Malaya, Burma, then Sumatra where these aircraft known as "Tojo" by the Allies, defended the vital oil fields at Palembang. *(S Hayashi)*

When the Pacific War broke out, these Nakajima Ki-49 Donryu heavy bombers were to replace the aging Ki-21 "Sallys". Allied personnel calling the Ki-49, "Helen", first encountered these Army bombers over New Britain and New Guinea. *(S Hayashi)*

As Japan's position deteriorated on the fighting scene, many aircraft were left behind as Allied forces advanced. Aircraft such as this "Tojo" and the "Nick" found on Clark Air Base in the Philippines were non-operational because of a poor supply system for even minor replacement parts. *(80-G-191802)*

## Kamikaze Tactics

Losses such as these could not be tolerated as a by-product of conventional warfare. A new means of causing destruction to the Allied forces had to be devised. It was during the Battle of Leyte Gulf that the Japanese for the first time used suicide attacks against surface ships on a planned basis and a substantial scale. Previously, there had been instances of isolated aircraft crashes on Allied ships, for the most part by aircraft which had been shot out of control.

It was not until the summer of 1944, after the loss of the Marianas, however, that the Japanese high command began to consider mass suicide crashes as a means of turning back the Allied advance. Thus began the third and final phase of the air war for Japan in its desperate attempt to stem the tide that would be the invasion of its home islands.

The first authenticated case of a pilot's announcing before take-off an intention to crash came on 15 October 1944 when Rear Admiral Arima made an abortive suicide attack on a US carrier force off Formosa. This zeal lit a spark of patriotic fervour, and suicide units began to be formed from regular Army and Navy air units in the Philippines. The first large attack by those units came on 25 October at the height of the fleet action. Considerable success was achieved; an escort carrier was sunk and several other vessels were damaged. Later, special suicide units were formed in Japan, mainly from the pilot training organizations, and before the Japanese withdrew from the Philippines, 650 suicide sorties were flown which scored 174 hits or damaging near misses on US surface vessels.

Even though Japanese combat aircraft in the Philippines at the beginning of the Mindoro operation, plus aircraft flown in as replacements, totalled more than 1,000, the Japanese were able to fly only about 750 sorties in defence against the two operations. Poor maintenance and lack of serviceable replacement parts was the cause. In order to resume lost effectiveness, almost every Japanese attack was planned to be executed as a suicide attack when it came to counter any US invasion. These attacks would continue to the end of the war in Japan's desperate attempt to repel the invasion of their home islands that they could see was certain.

The pending invasion became Japan's prime military concern. By mid-1945, nearly 8,000 kamikaze or special-attack aircraft were prepared for this invasion.[3] The Army provided 4,800 aircraft of this force and 5,900 came from the Navy.[4] All types were to be employed; fighters, bombers, reconnaissance, and even the slow and vulnerable fabric-covered biplane trainers. By late summer of that year, another 2,500 aircraft were expected to be converted to the kamikaze attack cause.

The Japanese counter attack plan of the invasion was to conserve this air strength until certain that the landing phase had begun. At that time, only a few hundred kamikaze sorties would be launched against the Allied carrier task forces supporting the invasion. Hoping to neutralize most of the Allied fleet defence system that was needed for a successful invasion against Japan, the bulk of the remaining kamikazes would be launched against the warships and particularly the transports while in the critical phase of boarding the assault barges in the invasion area. Within a ten-day period, Japanese defenders expected to completely expend these aircraft in a supreme effort to repel the invasion forces.

In August 1945, the greatest war of all time came to a conclusion. By mid-1945, in leading to this climax, the substance of Japan had been gutted; the best of its army and navy had been defeated; the Japanese Homeland was at the mercy of air raids and inevitable invasion. In the tradition of *bushido,* some military leaders were dedicated to fight to the very end to defend their Emperor and country. In this endeavour, nearly 10,700 aircraft[5] remained that would be used in this desperate effort to exert as much destruction against the invading forces as possible.

By the dropping of the atomic bomb, the war ended differently and with greater savings in lives on both sides than the planned invasion of the Japanese home islands. No longer was there the need for this frightful expenditure of human life and aircraft needed for the propaganda inspired "divine mission" of dying for the Emperor for the national cause. As the Allies went ashore with the hand of peace extended on both sides, it was this last ditch stand of surviving aircraft that the occupying forces found in a silent and non-flyable state when they arrived on Japanese soil.

Among the many types of kamikaze modified aircraft to be used in the final phase of the war were 1,750 Army trainers such as these Tachikawa Ki-9 "Spruce" intermediate trainers. Note 55 gal drum in rear cockpit filled with volatile fluid. Tail marking is of the 21st Wing. Photo was taken on 26 October 1945 at Kikuchi Airfield near Kumamoto, on Kyushu.

---

3: Reports of Gen. MacArthur, Vol 1. p.405.

4: Japanese Air Power, US Strategic Bombing Survey

5: Ibid.

A desperate situation is shown here as an attacking twin-engine "Nick" two-seat fighter barely misses a B-29 in this head on attack. The B-29 upper left is in trouble as it turns out of formation and trails smoke. *(USAF 58926 AC)*

The final phase of Japan's airpower was turned towards kamikaze attacks in a last ditch effort to slow the Allied advances. Seen here is a single Zero in a kamikaze attack the instant before it crashed into the battleship USS *Missouri* off Okinawa.

This Zero discovered by a TAIU team near Buna airstrip on New Guinea in 1943 was thought at first to be a new type fighter because of its squared-off wing tips. Removing aircraft from the jungle with obstacles such as this bomb crater were common problems for the TAIU teams.

# CHAPTER II
# THE PATH TO JAPAN

## Intelligence Teams at Work

Throughout the war years, there was a need by the Allies to learn all they could about Japanese equipment, production rates and distribution so that adequate counter-measures could be developed. There was also that continuing possibility that the Japanese, as well as the Germans, might have a technological breakthrough that could prove very useful to the Allies if detected through their intelligence network.

Although the war had ended, this need continued for sorting through the technology that was left intact within Japan. This consisted of gathering selected material, and moving it safely to the United States for further evaluation and study. This responsibility was shared by the US Navy, Army Air Forces, and members of the RAF.

Americans and Australians worked together in these recovery operations. Shown here is a Zero with its aft fuselage section removed, being moved to the shore for a barge shipment. Salvaged parts were initially taken to Brisbane, Australia for repair and flight testing.

Charged early in the war with this responsibility for gathering aviation related intelligence in the Pacific Area was the Technical Air Intelligence Unit (TAIU). This began early in 1943 as a small cadre in Melbourne, Australia, of US Air Force personnel, supplemented by Australians. As part of the 5th Air Force and Allied Air Forces, it served as a focal point for all air intelligence information. This intelligence network grew quickly, forming separate units in various parts of the Pacific and Asia. These were the teams that went into the jungles, in often hard-to-reach locations where downed Japanese aircraft had been reported. If the find was rare, labour-intensive efforts were made to disassemble and withdraw these aircraft for further study. The ultimate destination for this information was funnelled to the Technical Air Intelligence Center (TAIC) at Anacostia NAS in Washington, D.C., with Air Force interests located at Wright Field, near Dayton, Ohio.

Now with the cessation of hostile activities throughout the large expanse of the Pacific and Asia, the dispersed elements of the Technical Air Intelligence network; namely POA (Pacific Ocean Area), SEA (South-east Asia), China, India, along with SWPA (South-west Pacific Area) were now consolidated. This allowed their total resources to be concentrated under one central command for evaluations to be made in Japan, Korea and parts of China. Initially these units destined for Japan were to unite on Okinawa to prepare for that move. As it worked out, only the SWPA Unit actually went to Japan.

Natives to the islands were the main force of labour with aircraft recoveries. Here a "Betty" bomber nose is being rafted near Munda, New Georgia in February 1944 to a pick-up point. *(J H Lastly)*

This air view taken at an isolated corner of Clark Field, PI, soon after its liberation shows the collection of Japanese aircraft gathered here by the TAIU for their evaluation.

1.
Nakajima J1N1-S "Irving".

2.
Mitsubishi Ki-46 "Dinah".

3, & 4.
Kawasaki Ki-45 kai "Nick".

5, 6. & 7.
Kawasaki Ki-61 "Tony".

8.
Nakajima Ki-44 "Tojo".

9, & 10.
Nakajima Ki-84 "Frank".

11.
Kawanishi N1K1-J "George".

12, & 13.
Nakajima Ki-84 "Frank".

14.
Kawanishi N1K1-J "George".

15.
Nakajima Ki-44 "Tojo".

16, 17, & 18.
Kawasaki Ki-61 "Tony".

19.
Nakajima B6N2 "Jill".

20.
Kawanishi N1K1-J "George".

21.
Nakajima Ki-44 "Tojo".

22, 23 & 24.
Kawasaki Ki-45 "Nick".

25.
Nakajima B6N2 "Jill".

26.
Kawasaki Ki-45 "Nick".

27.
Mitsubishi G4M2 "Betty".

28.
Nakajima Ki-43 "Oscar".

The plan for locating, identifying and safeguarding this equipment found in Japan was started long before TAIU activities were moved to Japan. When rumours began that Japan had capitulated, this brought about renewed activity for the 129 team members of the TAIU at Clark AB in the Philippines, the unit that would have this task. It was essential that they be among the first to arrive in Japan in order to precede American troops and prevent them from stripping aircraft for souvenirs before their intelligence-gathering work was completed.

In this regard, one of the sayings often expressed by these intelligence gatherers was that "The Germans fought for *Hitler*, the Japanese fought for their *Emperor*, and the Americans fought for *souvenirs*." One of the most difficult tasks of these TAIU teams was to keep GIs away from captured enemy equipment. Americans have a fetish for souvenirs even though, once acquired, their interest level quickly dissipates. The hardest battles fought by TAIU personnel was often the cordoning off of captured Japanese aircraft. For even the most insignificant and minor bits and pieces of these machines could provide vital intelligence information.

For example: Metal identification nameplates, especially those from Japanese aircraft, their exotic oriental markings, were the first to disappear. They made ideal souvenirs to send in a letter to the folks back home. Yet, the data they revealed to intelligence teams was used to determine production rates and locations of key factories. Most importantly, this was often the only means of serial identification for a given aircraft, and once this was gone, the identity and related background of the aircraft could no longer be traced.

Another consideration was to initiate a plan to determine what Japanese equipment and materials, be it aircraft, engines, armament, or other related assemblies, were to be confiscated for Allied use and inspection. A query on this point was sent to the Technical Air Intelligence Center Headquarters in Washington. The questions were difficult ones to answer until the actual objects of interest could be examined. However, time lost in decision-making after their arrival on Japanese soil could jeopardize the safety of the aircraft that would eventually be acquired. To bridge this gap, the men at Clark established their own basic list of worthwhile items. It was based upon the knowledge they had already gained of Japan's various production aircraft types as well as those under development.

Team members of the TAIU anticipated that the list of aircraft would expand as unexpected aircraft were found. Four of each type, if available, would be the intended quantity. This would provide one aircraft each for the Army Air Forces, US Navy, RAF, and one spare. With this proposal sent to Washington, the reply was in full agreement, which set their planning action into motion. Eventually, this plan became a Supreme Command Allied Pacific (SCAP) Directive, AG45201, dated 12 September 1945, that ordered the Japanese government to assemble various types of Army and Navy aircraft to be sent to the United States.

The most important part of preparing Japanese aircraft for flying was to evaluate them against Allied aircraft and determine the best air tactics to use. This Nakajima Ki-84 "Frank" was evaluated against the Spitfire, Hellcat, and P-51 in the Philippines. *(80-G-193335)*

Another support aircraft used by the TAIU was this C-47 flown generally by the unit commander in the SW Pacific, then Lt-Col Frank McCoy, thus the name "The Real McCoy". McCoy was primarily responsible for Allied code names of Japanese aircraft.

When the TAI Units moved forward towards Japan, one of the few aircraft sent from the Philippines to the United States was this Nakajima Ki-84 "Frank". After passing through several owners, this aircraft now resides in Japan. *(80-G-413478)*

The Americans wasted no time in establishing themselves on the base almost within hours of their initial landing. For this operation of occupying Atsugi Air Base and surrounding areas, the tactical call sign for Atsugi became "Image Tower". *(SC 360763)*

At Clark AB, the TAI Unit quickly organized their equipment and packed it for the move. Most of the heavy equipment at Clark was trucked to an awaiting LST for the move to Okinawa. The remaining equipment and advance teams were flown to Okinawa, leaving behind the many Japanese aircraft the unit had been working on for so many months, preparatory to further flight evaluation. Seemingly, only one Japanese bomber and one fighter, a "Betty" and a "Frank", are known to have been sent to the United States of all the aircraft evaluated at Clark. At first glance, this seemed quite a loss of hundreds of man hours the mechanics had expended in making selected aircraft flyable, but greater treasures were expected ahead.

Only one of these enemy aircraft left behind survived for any appreciable time. It was an "Oscar II" that was placed on a pylon and mounted outside Base Operations at Clark. For a number of years this was a landmark for the many transients who moved through this busy Pacific crossroad. In time the war trophy was relocated to the Air Materiel Area on Clark Air Base, away from the mainstream of base activity. The aircraft remained in good condition and a point of interest to base personnel, but amidst cries of protest, it was taken down from its perch in 1960. The AMA Commander ordered it scrapped, even though organizations on the base were anxious to give it the care it deserved. Regrettably their efforts failed.

Meanwhile, on Okinawa, all available troop transports of the Far East Air Force had been mobilized for the mammoth air operations that would begin the occupation of Japan. Aircraft in greatest quantity were Curtiss C-46 Commandos, the largest twin-engine aircraft of the war, along with dozens of C-47 Skytrains and larger four-engined C-54 Skymasters. The initial target date for the move to Japan was postponed from 26 August, to 28 August, because of a typhoon in the area. When the weather improved, the greatest aerial movement during the Pacific War was begun.

At Atsugi airfield, twenty-seven miles south-west of the centre of Tokyo, several hundred Japanese aircraft lined the perimeter of the field, most having been stripped of their propellers. This was by Japanese decree as a precaution against their own air force personnel who protested the surrender and wished to make further flights that could be deemed hostile.

The Japanese did not expect the first American formations flying from Okinawa until 0900 hours, but half an hour earlier, a twin-engine aircraft appeared in the skies to the south. This was the first of an endless string of C-46 transports. The aircraft circled Atsugi and then made its approach from the south, touching down on an undamaged section of the runway at 0828 hours. It was followed by fourteen others which contained American soldiers and equipment for this initial group.

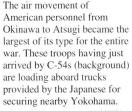

The air movement of American personnel from Okinawa to Atsugi became the largest of its type for the entire war. These troops having just arrived by C-54s (background) are loading aboard trucks provided by the Japanese for securing nearby Yokohama.
*(SC 210620-S)*

From the lead aircraft debarked a US Army colonel, who was in command of the advance party. Waiting automobiles transported him and his staff to the Japanese reception group at the edge of the field. Procedures that had been worked out with Japanese surrender envoys, who had gone to General MacArthur's headquarters in Manila on the night of 19 August, were beginning to take effect.

While this initial conference on Japanese soil was taking place, soldiers debarked from the transports coming onto the field every few minutes. Many contained Jeeps which were hastily unloaded, giving mobility to the exploratory parties being formed. A second flight of fifteen C-54s had all landed by 1100 hours. Navy F6F Hellcats and SB2C Helldivers that were circling overhead had escorted these transports that were carrying thirty officers and 120 men. All were wearing full combat equipment, and prepared for whatever might happen.

The Japanese were amazed at the efficiency with which these Navy fighters, that soon landed on the grass, quickly folded their wings "like cicadas", even while taxying to their parking positions. The Japanese made no attempt to conceal the degree to which they were impressed by the speed with which the Americans motorized themselves and investigated the entire field area. Their amazement was outspoken when within forty-five minutes after the first aircraft had touched down, portable Signal Corps transmitters were on the air establishing communications with the base they had departed on Okinawa through their radio relay in an aircraft overhead. Thirty-eight troop transport aircraft followed, carrying protective combat forces, necessary supplies of fuel, lubricants, and maintenance equipment. This made the intrepid advanced unit self-sustaining until the anticipated arrival two days later of the main airborne force which constituted the first of the occupation troops for Japan.

After the runway and base support facilities had been repaired by Japanese labour, the base was ready for operation. By the end of the first day of transporting the actual Occupation Forces to Japan, 4,200 troops and 123 aircraft had completed the move from Okinawa. Among those arriving at Atsugi were investigative team members of the Technical Air Intelligence Unit. Day after day the transports shuttled more troops and support equipment into Atsugi. From there, they fanned out over the countryside to take control of their pre-designated areas. By 4 September, American forces had control of all the major airfields in and around the Tokyo Area.

In concert with this operation, one TAIU team landed on Kyushu, while another moved into Korea. The search for Japanese technology was on. This would last over the next three months until the gathered materials would be on their way to the United States and the clean-up of military hardware would nearly be concluded.

This view of vast quantities of derelict Japanese aircraft is what Americans saw around the perimeter of the field as they arrived at Atsugi Air Base. Debris in the foreground is a bombed out hangar. Army C-47s are in the background.
*(C-58946 AC)*

This area of Atsugi Air Base was referred to as the bone yard. These unserviceable aircraft were made even more so by having been pushed into this area by bulldozers to make room for American aircraft. Many types of Japanese Naval aircraft can be identified here.

The ramp on which these Japanese fighters were once placed has been rapidly cleared with no concern for the damage the method used would cause. Seen here are a "Zeke" (Zero), a "Myrt", "Jack", "Frances" and a "Grace".

The Japanese government was well aware of the possibility of retaliatory air attacks that might be made after the surrender by some Japanese pilots that felt strongly about continuing the war. To preclude this happening, the Japanese Military leaders ordered that all but certain aircraft be rendered non-flyable. How this was done is clearly evident in this picture.

James P Gallagher has captured with his camera the many views of this defeated air force as seen by Americans that arrived at Atsugi Air Base in that first month of the Occupation. Perhaps there is no better film coverage of that situation than these pictures by Gallagher, contained in this chapter. Having lost his good camera in an emergency water landing, he resorted to a 120 film size folding No 1 Pocket Kodak f-6.3, 1/50th camera sent from his parents' attic.

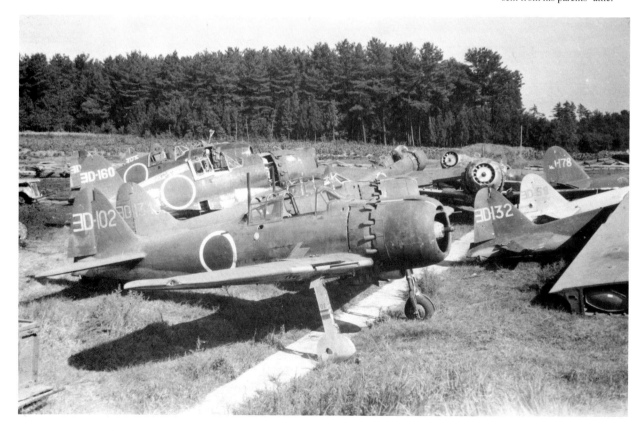

# CHAPTER III
# MEATBALLS AND DEAD BIRDS

## At the Hands of the Occupation Forces

This photograph centres upon the bulldozer in the foreground carting off this "Nell" bomber to the scrap heap. Imagine the agonizing sound of scraping, tearing metal as this twisting of aircraft took place as they were pushed and dragged to their doom.

When these first Americans arrived at Atsugi on this first day, they were amazed by the hoards of former enemy aircraft that heavily stocked the airfield. "Meatballs were everywhere," as one GI recalled when seeing all the aircraft, using the term the Allies applied to any sighting of a Japanese aircraft, referring to their red-disk *Rising Sun* insignia as a meatball. These were *dead birds* for sure because each had been rendered impotent by one form or another; deliberately damaged flight controls, propeller removed, or flattened tyres. This once lethal force of various types of combat aircraft at Atsugi were as silenced as a flock of birds struck by lightning.

There was good reason for this neutralizing action that was initiated by the Japanese before the arrival of the Occupying Forces. Some factions within the Japanese military were not willing to accept the Emperor's personal radio broadcast message of 15 August, announcing the surrender decision. Not only had a *coup d'état* been planned by young officers in the War Ministry and the Army General Staff, but extremist elements of the Navy protested as well. Aircraft from the 302nd Kokutai (Air Group) based at Atsugi, flew over the surrounding area and scattered leaflets urging continuation of the war on the grounds that the surrender edict was not the true will of the Emperor. To further disrupt the surrender, the commander of this Kokutai threatened to intercept the Emperor's surrender envoys in flight as they passed Atsugi on their first segment to MacArthur's Manila headquarters on 19 August. A circuitous route was taken by the transporting aircraft, flown with radios silenced. However, the Kokutai commander, upon seeing that he was not fully supported by his officers, committed *hari-kari* the night before.

In light of this, an edict was levied by those in power within the Japanese government, that no Japanese military aircraft would be flown after 1800 hours on 24 August. To enforce this rule, serviceable aircraft were to be rendered non-airworthy, but by the terms of the surrender negotiations, arms (including aircraft) were not to be destroyed in advance of the Occupation Forces.

The awaited day for the start of the occupation of Japan by the Allies came on 28 August 1945 when the first Americans began landings on Honshu, the main island of Japan. What could have been the world's most bloody invasion, became, instead, one of peace because of Japan's capitulation and co-operation. On that day between 0828 and 1100 hours, a small airborne advance party of 150 communications specialists and engineers alighted at Atsugi Airfield, the foothold for the Occupation Forces was established, some twenty odd miles south-west of Tokyo.

This A6M5c "Zeke", "Yo" D-127, appears to be complete and ready for duty. It is possible that the seat has been removed and is resting at the rear of the aircraft. Wing gun bay hatch is open and the trailing edge of the wing tip is missing.

MEATBALLS AND DEAD BIRDS 43

This view of "Yo"D-127 gives a clear picture of the wing-gun installation of two 20 mm cannon inboard and two Type 3 13 mm machine guns outboard on the "Zeke" fighter. Adding to this firepower was the addition of under-wing racks to accommodate small air-to-air rocket bombs. This armament configuration identifies this model of the Zero Fighter as being an A6M5c.

Zero Fighter "Yo"D-127 was an ideal one for this camera view because it appeared so complete and ready for flight compared to the damage and destruction of other aircraft around it.

The daring little group began immediately to set up the communications and other operational facilities for the swarms of transport aircraft that would bring the 11th Airborne Division to Atsugi to establish the American airhead at this base. Over the next few days, the aircraft ramps had to be cleared of Japanese aircraft for the incoming transports bringing in the initial occupation forces. MacArthur's Air Guard of Honor, the 49th Fighter Group with its three squadrons of P-38s, would be the first Air Force combat unit assigned to Japan and had a need for ground space as well. To accomplish this, any means available for removing the Japanese aircraft, whether to be towed or merely pushed with bulldozers were to be used to clear the parking space.

Much of this clearing was yet to be done when elements of this 49th Fighter Group began arriving a few days after the first Americans touched down at Atsugi. Among this advance party was the 7th Squadrons Communications Officer, 1st Lt James P Gallagher, who had arrived by LST from Okinawa. Gallagher was a prolific, and prize-winning photographer in his own right, with an eye for capturing the unusual. Certainly, the aircraft and the conditions found at Atsugi were in the unusual category at this historic time of the occupation. During times that his unit duties were satisfied, Gallagher, who was one of the very early camera-weilding servicemen, set about exploring the base and photographing aircraft in particular. On weekends, adventuresome trips with friends by jeep were made to other airfields around the Tokyo area for capturing on film the rare aircraft seen at those locations. Gallagher recognized that he was witnessing a rare window of time in the history of World War II, and appropriately recorded on film almost every aircraft type he saw to the limits of his dwindling film supply.

Resting beside this Zero A6M5c in the background is one of its intended replacements, the Mitsubishi J2M3 "Jack" fighters which has a four-bladed propeller turned by a powerful 1,800 hp Kasei engine.

Somewhat isolated from the other aircraft on Atsugi Air Base is this earlier model of the Zero, an A6M2. To enable the early Zeros with their 39 ft 4 in wing span to have more deck elevator clearance aboard Japanese aircraft carriers, only the outer portion of the wing tips would fold. This saved structural weight as opposed to having the entire wing fold as was done with American Navy fighters in an effort to save hangar deck space aboard the carriers.

For the years that followed, Gallagher's photographs satisfied his personal memories of those early days in Japan. In later years, recognizing the budding interest in Japanese aviation that had languished for nearly two decades after the war, he produced a book in small quantity titled *Meatballs and Dead Birds,* containing these photographs along with his impressions, a book that is now a classic. It is within this and the next chapter that most of these photographs reappear for only the second time. They, along with additional photos, clearly show the condition of the Japanese aircraft found at Atsugi and other Tokyo area airfields. Some of these aircraft have modifications that make them one of a kind and not otherwise recorded.

Relating to these pictures and experiencing the early days of the Occupation Forces in Japan, Gallagher describes Atsugi as having been considered by the Japanese military the most important air base in the Tokyo area. There were close to 400 aircraft there at the end of the war. When the 49th arrived, according to Gallagher, most of the Japanese aircraft were in some way disabled. Because of this, only aircraft in seemingly wrecked condition, or at least incomplete, were available for photographing.

In the descriptions of the aircraft about to follow, the Allied code system names will be used for simplicity. This naming system was developed early in the war when it became apparent that Allied airmen found the Japanese identities not only complicated and confusing, but often difficult to pronounce and understand in radio transmissions. To solve this problem, a code system was established whereby each Japanese fighter and floatplane was given a familiar boy's name, while bombers, flying-boats, and reconnaissance aircraft were given easy-to-pronounce girls' names.

Of the aircraft types most readily seen at Atsugi, there were dozens of defending fighters such as "Jacks" and Zero fighters, code-named "Zekes". Fighters were plentiful since this was the primary defence base of the Navy for the Tokyo and Yokohama area. Also in large numbers were "Irvings," "Frances" and "Judys". There were a few "Bettys", "Nells", "Vals" and "Myrts" on hand, plus many training and transport aircraft. Four "Baka Bombs" stood in readiness in concrete revetments at one of the edges of the field.

By American air base standards at that time for large fields of this type, according to Gallagher, the base at Atsugi was relatively primitive. There was one paved strip of about 5,000 feet with a parallel taxiway. There were some paved aprons in the hangar areas; however, they were small in number and size. Some of the hangars had dirt floors and were unfinished, framed-up but having no roof. Some of these missing roof coverings, it was learned later, had been deliberately removed so that concussions from the increased bombing attacks would not cause as much structural damage to the buildings or have the roof particles become flying debris.

"Some of us of the 49th," Gallagher recounts, "would watch the field being cleared to make room for the incoming US air power. Many types of Japanese Navy aircraft were being literally shoved aside and ripped apart, yet no one at the time felt much about it . . . after all, these had been war weapons that had been used against us! I have since wondered what it would have been like had the situation been reversed?"

What was seen at Atsugi is best told by the many photographs that were taken during these early days of the Occupation. These aircraft, like those at many air bases throughout Japan and her formerly occupied territories, were the Japanese aircraft survivors of that conflict, yet many were to meet an ignominious death at the business end of a bulldozer's blade.

Another Zero A6M2 is certainly in no condition to fly with the absence of its wheels, propeller and tail cone. A fairing of the right stabilizer hangs loose and the wing tips are partially folded. When aboard carriers these wing tips were folded manually by deck crews. This aircraft has tail unit-number 741, identifying it as being from the 51st Koku Sentai.

This is an unusual Zero in that it is a two-seat trainer version of the A6M2 early series. Most were without the wheel cover fairing as shown here. The stabilizing fins attached to the side of the fuselage were to aid in spin recovery. This version was also used for target towing for fighter units. A Nakajima B6N2 "Jill" is in the background.

This is a line of Mitsubishi Raiden fighters that the Allies code named "Jack". These were designed as air defence interceptors. They were a formidable attacker as any B-29 crew member will attest.

Rare for Japanese aircraft was this turbo-supercharger on the later version of "Jack", the J2M4 Raiden. This allowed the aircraft to reach 314 knots at 30,185 ft, a performance far in excess of other defending Japanese fighters.

Had it not been for the shortage of fuel and a rather high maintenance-down rate, many more encounters would have occurred with these "Jacks" against the B-29 raids. They were considered to be the best of all fighters against the big bombers. This trio of "Jacks" was assigned to the 302nd Kokutai, identified by the tail mark "Yo"D.

The clean lines of this otherwise very stocky fighter are not only broken by the missing cowling, but the absence of the pointed tail cone. This J2M3 version of the Raiden was produced in the largest quantity of all variance, totalling 260 machines.

Members of the 49th Fighter Group to which photographer Gallagher belonged, decided to add a Mitsubishi J2M3 "Jack" to their stable of P-38 Lightnings. As one of the American crew chiefs excused this action, "MacArthur doesn't have to know about it". A bulldozer is being attached for the tow recovery.

The intrepid Americans tow the "Jack" to the safe haven of the hangar used by the 49th Fighter Group. There were no major plans made for the aircraft, but the clean lines of this fighter design made it worth the effort to save for the squadron.

For a while at least, it was rewarding for the Americans to have a "new toy" for their unit to have in their midst. There were plenty of other "Jack" fighters around that would yield the missing parts to make the aircraft complete.

As the "point-system" allowed many Americans of the Occupation Forces to return home, replacement personnel were less interested in what had taken place before their arrival, and this "Jack" was destined to meet the same fate as the other aircraft by ending up in the heap of scrap metal at Atsugi.

Unlike other Japanese single engine fighters of both Army and Navy, the "Jack" had by far the roomiest cockpit of them all. To some pilots, this wide canopy was felt to be a hindrance to their visibility.

This Mitsubishi "Jack" was found nestled in one of about ten grotto-like hangars that were built in one area of Atsugi as was the case at many other bases. They were relatively bomb proof and difficult to see from the air because of the natural flora covering.

An unusual aircraft to find was this and a few other Aichi D3A2 "Val" dive bombers. Its fixed gear made it appear out of place at the time of Japan's surrender since more advanced aircraft were in strong evidence. The "Val" was already considered obsolete at the time they participated in the dive bomber force for the attack upon Pearl Harbor, yet it was very effective. Tail code is that of the 1081st Kokutai.

This closer view of "Val" shows it draped with a camouflage netting that must have been used to conceal this aircraft at some remote point around Atsugi from where it was towed for consolidating all Japanese aircraft. Outdated and unserviceable aircraft of this type may have been used as airfield decoys against Allied air attacks.

The backbone of the Japanese Navy's bomber force was the Mitsubishi G4M Type 1 Attack Bomber, code-named "Betty". Among the many aircraft to be destroyed at Atsugi was this pair of "Bettys" that survived the many air attacks by Allied fighter sweeps.

The gun barrel has been removed from this 20 mm cannon in the turret of "Betty". This was but one of the defending guns aboard "Betty" bombers that made the outcome of any attack by an Allied fighter more than a small risk.

The "Betty" carried a respectable bomb load for an extended distance. Its main drawback was its lack of sufficient armour protection for its crew and fuel tanks. This made them very vulnerable when attacked by Allied fighters.

This "Betty" appears to have been stripped of all useful components including its engines. As such, it was used as a decoy for attacking Allied fighters against Atsugi. Note the wooden paddles tied in place to appear as propellers.

This is the business end of the "Betty" bomber where the bombardier sat. This nose dome, although shattered, served as a mount for a flex-mounted 7.7 mm Type 92 machine gun. The nose rotated by hand to position the gun port in the most advantageous firing location.

Any aircraft that could be made airworthy was considered to be part of the kamikaze attacks when the expected main Allied invasion was to begin. This "Betty" appears to be fairly complete and possibly serviceable by having retained both of its propellers.

Framed in the open hatch of this "Betty" bomber is the photographer of pictures contained in this chapter and part of the next, Lieutenant Jim Gallagher. His pictures taken at Atsugi capture what was seen by the Occupation Forces in September and October 1945.

This view creates a feeling of helplessness in seeing these "Bettys" and other aircraft pushed over the embankment and clinging precariously to the slope. Off the port wing is the only example found at Atsugi of a Kawanishi "George" fighter, a type said to be conspicuous by its absence according to photographer Gallagher.

Another twin-engine aircraft found in large numbers at Atsugi was the Nakajima J1N1 Gekko, having as its code name, "Irving". Its initial intent was that of a twin-engine escort fighter for deep penetration sorties into China. Luckily for the builder, the Zero went into service first and filled this job, for the "Irving" was plagued with development problems.

The "Irving" became an excellent night fighter by May 1943 with a newly-developed night air attack system. Two 20 mm cannon were mounted obliquely behind the crew compartment as seen in this photograph. With a gun-sight pointed upwards at the same angle, the pilot trailed beneath the bombers that were silhouetted against the brighter overhead sky and made the firing attack without having to adjust for lead or lag.

This spherical turret was a Nakajima refinement of the French design and was installed in limited production of reconnaissance "Irvings". Note the streamlining changes behind the pilot's canopy, and the elongated canopy aft of the turret. Both types of turrets carried a single 20 mm cannon.

This closer look at the gun turret suggests that it is a derivation of the French de Boysson-type gun turret, a type initially installed on G5N Shinzan "Liz", four-engine bombers.

This photograph of an "Irving" at Atsugi shows not only the clear nose cone but the flat glass panels beneath the nose that were added for the night fighter configuration. With a large opening in the instrument panel in which a second gun-sight was mounted, the pilot could sight downward at 30 degrees for firing the ventral gun. This armament arrangement was not only used against aircraft but light shipping as well.

This closer view of "Irving" not only shows the two upper 20 mm cannon, but it has two 20 mm cannon pointed downward at the standard 30 degree angle. For overhead attacks, a gunsight mounted in the instrument panel was directed down through glass panels in the nose for sighting. Note that the rear canopy has been replaced with metal, undoubtedly because of muzzle blast near breakable plastic and to minimize the flash within the cockpit.

Another "Jill" that seems intact is crowded in among many other aircraft at Atsugi. Note the side-looking radar antenna along the side of the aft fuselage. The top portion of the windshield could be hinged upwards for ground and deck taxying since the pilot seat could be raised above the windshield level for better visibility while on the surface.

This "Myrt" had its gear collapsed while it was being pushed to this area of Atsugi Air Base. This view emphasized the long slender lines and the lengthy canopy for three crew members of this fast aircraft. A number of these reconnaissance aircraft had been modified by having an oblique gun mounted in the rear cockpit for B-29 interceptions at night. Others were used for kamikaze missions.

A close cousin to the "Jill" was this Nakajima C6N1 Saiun. Known as "Myrt" to the Allies. These sleek, pencil thin reconnaissance aircraft could operate at very high altitudes and at great speed. Intercepting fighters were given quite a challenge in catching "Myrt". Aside from the damaged stabilizer tip, note the angle-off marks painted on the stabilizer for calculating wind drift angles.

"Judy" was a replacement aircraft for the "Val" as a dive bomber. Aside from one other Navy aircraft, the Seiran, this Kugisho D4Y2 Suisei was unusual for Japanese aircraft in having an in-line water-cooled engine. This Atsuta 32 engine was a version of the German DB 600-series, 1,400 hp engine built under licence by Aichi.

This picture shows the installation of the obliquely mounted 20 mm cannon in the rear compartment of a "Judy". This was the Type I cannon (Ho-5) having a rate of fire of 850 rpm and a muzzle velocity of 2,400 feet per second. This weapon had an effective range of up to 2,950 feet.

There were no end of problems with the Atsuta engine. To increase the effectiveness of this good aircraft design of "Judy", it was modified so that later production aircraft would be fitted with the air-cooled Kinsei radial engine having 1,560 hp.

No care was taken by the Americans when moving this and other aircraft to a distant corner of Atsugi. Seemingly this "Judy" was pushed at its side which collapsed its landing gear. Obviously configured for kamikaze attack, everything in its rear cockpit had been removed for the planned one-way mission.

Dimensionally, "Judy" was a little larger than the standard Japanese fighters. This warplane possessed remarkable speeds in all its models, but was severely short on protection of the crew and fuel tanks. The bomb bay doors for carrying bombs internally are apparent as are the wing racks.

An exceptional late-war Navy bomber was this Yokosuka P1Y1 Ginga, code named "Frances". This aircraft was as large as contemporary twin-engine bombers, but the crew was limited to three, contrary to Japanese customs of a large crew for many gun positions. The colour on this "Frances" was unusual in that it was an earthen green-brown on the upper surfaces and a light grey on the bottom areas. The Hinomarus' white outlines were all hidden by the repainting of their normal red with a rust colour that was carried beyond the previous border. Note how flat the finish was for this aircraft, with no signs of lustre anywhere.

The camouflage colours applied to "Frances" aircraft varied widely. This aircraft was a little brighter green than most of its companion aircraft. The rather poor paint job had weathered too fast, letting much of the bright aluminium show, giving the plane a strange and almost truculent look. The number 181 on its tail was painted over from the former 305 which seemed appropriate for its earlier unit. The 3 of 305 signified torpedo bomber, a designed mission for these aircraft.

This photograph gives a close detailed look at the nicely streamlined crew compartment of "Frances". Also apparent is the deadly muzzle of the cannon which is mounted behind the rear compartment. The shock of the muzzle blast must have been something to remember when seated in rear or even the front cockpit on a night, B-29 interception mission.

The one "Liz" found at Atsugi by the Americans was too heavy to be moved by available equipment, so its destruction was begun on site. Selective dynamiting began the job until reduced to sizes small enough to move.

The unusual presence of a seaplane at a land base was this Nakajima E8N Reconnaissance seaplane "Dave". Date of photo was 5 September 1945. These aircraft served the Japanese fleet very early in the war being catapulted from cruisers and battleships.

The north-west corner of Atsugi appeared to be a safe haven for many of the aircraft initially. Although indignantly pushed together in no sense of order, it was here that most of the fairly intact aircraft remained for a brief period. Note the haste with which the numbers were painted on the "Jill", "Val" and "Judy" in the foreground, denoting their unit as the 108st Kokutai. These aircraft were used as decoys or for coastal shipping surveillance.

As was to be expected, the most numerous aircraft type to be encountered at Atsugi was the Zero Fighter, code named "Zeke". Except for the missing propeller, this Mitsubishi A6M5c appears to be complete. The tail code "Yo"D-102 identifies the unit as the 302nd Naval Air Group.

This view is of "Zeke" "Yo"D-102 with discarded Japanese trucks placed nearby. On the airfield ramp behind are Curtiss C-46 Commandos of the 2nd and 433rd Troop Carrier Groups that ferried troops and supplies to Atsugi from Okinawa. An interim control tower has been built on the roof of the building in the background.

There were two production configurations for the fuselage of "Irving". Those like the above were designed to carry two turret barbettes in the aft section when first envisioned as an escort fighter. When the barbette arrangement was abandoned, later models had the crew reduced to two, having its aft fuselage without the pronounced step.

The "Irvings" that were stationed at Atsugi were a lethal weapon for the attacking B-29s to reckon with. Flying in the darkness below the B-29, they were very difficult to see. For the night interceptor role, these aircraft were painted black-green, top and bottom.

The tail code of this "Irving" was undoubtedly "Yo"D-172, identifying it as belonging to the 2nd Hikotai, 302nd Kokutai. Codes of units assigned directly to the Yokosuka Naval District used the katakana symbol "Yo" (backward E) for Yokosuka, followed by a distinguishing Roman alphabet letter that was allotted sequentially in accordance with the chronological order in which units were directly assigned to the Yokosuka Naval District. The 302nd Kokutai being the fourth unit so assigned, carried the unit code "Yo"D.

This Nakajima B6N2 Tenzan, code named "Jill", may have been left operational from outward appearances. These carrier-based torpedo bombers were pressed into massive suicide missions in the closing months of the war, and others were awaiting modification for that purpose.

Although "Judy" was the fastest carrier-borne dive-bomber in service during World War II and of any country, the purpose for this aircraft being at Atsugi was twofold. This one has been modified as a night fighter with one obliquely-mounted gun in the rear compartment for use as an interceptor of B-29s. Further inspection revealed that it was also modified to be a kamikaze aircraft when that time came.

The tail codes seen on "Frances" of the 302nd Kokutai are interesting in that they begin with a "1", which normally signified the aircraft to be a land-based fighter. In this case the "1" is believed to denote 2nd Hikotai of the 302 Kokutai.

A Yagi antenna mast protrudes from the nose of this P1Y1 "Frances" behind which is the opened crew entry hatch. Side facing antenna can be seen along the aft fuselage. The bomb bay is also open, revealing that the doors move inside the fuselage rather than protrude into the wind stream and thus eliminating a maximum speed for having the bomb-doors open.

Atsugi held surprises at every turn in its early days of occupation. Here is the fuselage of an American Douglas Boston III (A-20) that was flown and tested by the Japanese. Twenty Bostons were shipped to Java for the Netherlands Air Force, but were captured by the Japanese while still in their crates at the unloading docks at Tijilatjap Harbour. More than one is believed to have been test-flown in Japan.

Similar occurrences took place with other American equipment that was captured by the Japanese. Here is one of several Curtiss P-40s taken into custody by the Japanese, probably from the Netherlands East Indies. A Japanese-flown P-40 was used in an aerial gunnery training film for the Japanese Navy just as Americans did with captured Japanese aircraft.

This "Tony" was of one ideally set apart from the others for a good camera perspective. Its flamboyant colours and markings were similar to those of German aircraft in the First World War. Like the other "Tonys" found at Chofu that had the blotch-type camouflage (with the one exception), they were basically unpainted dull dural aluminium on which was added medium green splotches of various shapes and sizes. The green splotches were on the upper surfaces and fully around the fuselage in the area behind the wing's trailing edge. The lower area of the front of the fuselage as well as the under surfaces of the wing and tail were left unpainted.

The markings for this "Tony" were quite colourful as were most of the others found at Chofu. The vertical tail was the same red as the Hinomaru, with a bright yellow flashing thunderbolt unit marking. In front of the tail a tri-colour band of yellow, white and red which ringed the fuselage. A striking orange-red lightning streak ran from the nose to the cockpit with a sufficient margin from the green splotches to not interrupt its lines. What seemed a strange colour for drop tanks, these were painted yellow.

This transport aircraft photographed at Chofu in September 1945 appears to be in flying condition, its doors open awaiting passengers and crew that never came. This was known as the Mitsubishi Ki-57 "Topsy", a passenger version of the much used Mitsubishi Ki-21 bomber, code named "Sally". The Japanese Army Air Force used "Sally" extensively over China and in limited numbers in the early stages of the Pacific War. "Topsys" were the standard transports for the Japanese Army. A civil version was the MC-20 built for and operated by Dai Nippon Koku KK.

Aircraft of the types shown here wre unusual at Irumagawa AB that was dedicated to the Army's air academy for student officers and pilot training. It can be assumed that these aircraft were among the many that were dispersed and held in readiness for the expected invasion for which they would have been used as kamikaze aircraft. Seen here is a Ki-54 "Hickory" (left), Ki-46 "Dinah" (centre), Ki-48 "Lili" and Ki-55 "Ida".

Another "oldie" was the remains of this Mitsubishi A5M "Claude", long retired from front-line service when the Pacific War began. It was probably used at Atsugi as a training aid for ground crews.

This bomber was another early-war aircraft of the Japanese Navy. Known as "Nell" by the Allies, these bombers were the main driving force in the air war over China and the opening phase of the Pacific War. Removed from front-line Pacific War action early in the operation, this "Nell" served in a bomber training unit, identified by its tail letters that read "ToYo" for Toyohashi Kokutai.

Unbelievable, but it was true –
at the bottom of the pile at the
left and top right are Nakajima
A4N1 biplane fighters, a type
that first entered Navy service
in 1936 and replaced a year
later by the "Claude"
monoplane fighter. Had these,
along with others perhaps,
been included in the count of
2,700 "trainer biplanes" that
were mustered for the planned
kamikaze attacks? At the top,
facing the camera is an
"Irving" twin-engined night
fighter.

These were dangerous
weapons – particularly to the
pilots that flew them. These
were the Ohka Kamikaze
human-guided bombs. The two
Ohka found at Atsugi were
housed in grotto-type shelters.
Undoubtedly these were
positioned for the final Allied
assault on the home islands.
They had proven themselves
as a deadly weapon in the
Okinawan campaign.

Although this is a Japanese built Navy transport, it had lines familiar to most people. It was a Showa-built Navy Type L2D3 known more popularly by the Allies as "Tabby". This was a licence-built Douglas DC-3 with modifications made by the Japanese Navy. These changes not only included light armament as the gun blister at the top will show, but windows were added in the crew compartment area. This type of aircraft was powered with 1,300 hp Mitsubishi Kensei engines, which, interestingly, provided more power than those engines used in the American counterpart.

The collapse of this hangar and the crush of the aircraft inside was so symbolic of the destruction and end of Japan's air forces. (USAAF 59077 AC)

Tachikawa Air Base as it was photographed on 28 August 1945, the day the first Occupation Forces arrived at Atsugi Air Base 18 miles to the south. The military side of the base is at the left of the bomb-cratered runway and parking ramp. Some aircraft can be seen parked in separate locations on the ramp and grass area. At the right is the industrial and military laboratory section of the base. Today, west (left) of the hangar line, the former building area is the Showa Memorial Park which includes a recreational lake. The flying field remains with its old but resurfaced 4,500-foot runway 01-19 supplemented with a parallel 5,000-foot runway.

# CHAPTER IV

# EXPEDITIONS TO OTHER AIR BASES

## Surprises in Many Forms

As the Americans continued to gain mutual confidence with their former enemy, particularly while now on the home soil of the Japanese, this ease in relationships led to driving excursions away from their home base. For some, this was to see other Japanese airfields and the interesting aircraft they held in store. Primarily these were the major airfields around the Tokyo area that were not only used in the day-to-day air defence of this heartland of Japan and were to be the key bases in the expected invasion, but some were development and logistic centres for the Imperial Japanese Army and Navy air forces. These bases were the resting places for hundreds of Japanese aircraft and although the wrecking crews almost immediately began to collect them into scrap piles, there were enough aircraft remaining for curious American GIs to inspect, photograph and cannibalize for souvenirs over the next eighteen months following the surrender.

One of these frequent weekend adventurers of the early occupation recorded his memories of these excursions. According to C M Daniels of the 8th Photo Reconnaissance Squadron stationed at Chofu AB at the time, a typical weekend consisted of getting a jeep from the motor pool, some beer at the Post Exchange and begging, borrowing or stealing some grub from the mess sergeant and *taking off*. Destinations were not always planned, merely a direction in hopes of coming across an airfield with its unique treasures to be discovered. Roads were narrow, dusty, and with luck, would be gravel. Aside from pot holes, obstacles were often bicycles with goods stacked upon them with what seemed to be half of that person's worldly belongings. Generally, their owners could only push and steer the heavily-laden bicycle, and would willingly scramble out of the way and wait for the passing of any powered vehicle.

Then there were the all-too-familiar Japanese odours of the countryside, Daniels clearly recalls. The 'honey dippers' carrying their cargoes of abominable stench to the fields for fertilizing, the eternal wood-burning smell in the air, the peculiar aroma of a small town just passed through. The never-to-be-duplicated noises of squeaking and clanking of narrow gauge railway trains entering a station as you pass by, and the chatter of people negotiating with shopkeepers in the open food markets are memories never to be forgotten.

Locating any of these air bases was normally met by surprise over such success. The Japanese were masters in their use of dispersal revetments and camouflage. They were ingenious in making use of local materials for camouflage. Bamboo was plentiful, as was rice straw, and these materials were widely used in building camouflage shelters to conceal aircraft revetments.

James P Gallagher with camera in hand, not only extensively photographed aircraft at Atsugi as seen in the previous chapter, but roamed several of these air bases within the flat area around Tokyo known as the Kanto Plains. He captured many of the aircraft on film as they were first seen by the advancing Americans. Other rare and unusual pictures of aircraft supplement his work in this chapter.

The early vertical photographic coverage of selected airfields are samples of the type of photography taken daily, weather permitting, from a time shortly before the surrender until the Allies had secured these bases on the ground. From these photographs, any marshalling of aircraft by the Japanese could be detected from the pictures. Those views used in this chapter were taken on the day the Allies first arrived at Atsugi, 28 August 1945 by F-7s (B-24s) of the 20th Reconnaissance Squadron, 6th Reconnaissance Group flying from Okinawa.

***Tachikawa Air Base:*** A popular destination for a day's adventuring was Tachikawa Air Base because of its huge US Post Exchange in comparison to other bases. This base could best be described as having been the air matériel centre for the Imperial Japanese Air Force and the USAAF was converting it for their similar needs. This base was located fourteen air miles due north of Atsugi, and sixteen miles in a straight line west of Tokyo, with all measurements relevant to the Imperial Palace. Tachikawa had housed the Rikugun Kokugijutsu Kenkyujo (Army Aeronautical Research Institute), the Dia-Ichi Rikugun Kokusho (First Army Air Arsenal) as well as the Tachikawa Hikoki K.K. (Tachikawa Aeroplane Co. Ltd.) to name a few of its tenants.

Chofu Air Base on the west edge of Tokyo was the Army's main air defence base for Tokyo as Atsugi AB was for the Japanese Navy. The aircraft found in greatest numbers at Chofu were the Kawasaki Ki-61 Hien, code named "Tony". The flashy tail marking identifies their unit as being the 244th Fighter Sentai. This particular "Tony" found at Chofu was the only one that had a base coat of snowy white over-painted with blotches of olive-green all around the fuselage and on the upper wing and tail surfaces. The bottom of the wings and tail surfaces were all white. A six-inch bright yellow band circled the fuselage in front of the tail of the plane. The flashing thunder on the tail was a flaming red to the first star, at which place it became a bright orange colour. The number 66 on the wheel covers was painted black.

*(J Gallagher)*

This air base became the hub of activities during the early occupation because of its logistic support for Air Force activities throughout the Far East. FEAMCOM (Far East Air Matériel Command) became an often-used acronym, for it was the air depot for servicing all types of aircraft used throughout the Far East, employing indigenous labour, many of whom were well-trained, having worked in the Japanese aircraft factories during the war. A Troop Transport Wing, and later a headquarters for an Air Division also took residence there for many years of American occupancy that followed.

***Chofu Air Base:*** Halfway into Tokyo from Tachikawa was Chofu Air Base, once a very crucial Army airfield for the air defence of Tokyo. Stationed there were the 52nd Sentai with its Ki-84 "Franks", and the 244th Sentai which operated "Tonys", both the in-line engine Ki-61 and the radial Ki-100 varieties. Examples of Mitsubishi Ki-46 "Dinahs" were the remnants of the 17th Sentai for their reconnaissance mission. Supposedly not considered operationally assigned to the Army were the suicide mission Ki-115 Tsurugi special purpose attackers, of which a few were found dispersed around the field. The greatest find on the airfield was the experimental Nakajima Ki-87 heavy fighter of which only this one was completed in April 1945. Further development rested with Nakajima's nearby Mitaka Engine Research Works in resolving problems with the turbo-supercharger. Chofu AB was its flight-test facility.

Chofu remained an active airfield through the occupation, at first for light military aircraft, then for flying clubs. In the late 1950s, much of the flying field was taken over for the construction of family housing for US Forces Japan and became known as Kanto Mura (Village) Family Housing Annex.

Victory markings on Japanese aircraft were no more uncommon than on American aircraft of the Pacific War. The quantity on this "Tony" seen at Chofu was worth recording through Jim Gallagher's camera. The custom was to credit the aircraft, as well as the pilot since few had their own assigned aircraft. This "Tony" was painted a "chocolate bar" brown all over, with unusually brilliant red Hinomaru insignia. Most remarkably, a large "Kelly-green" Shamrock was painted on both sides of the fuselage. These brightest-of-greens shamrocks were bordered in white. The vertical tail surface had the insignia of the 244th Sentai painted in white, and a five-inch band of white around the fuselage in front of the tail surfaces. *(J Gallagher)*

This transport version, of what the Allies called "Hickory", was a design that was quite versatile in the Japanese Army. Built by Tachikawa as the Ki-54, its manufacturing that began in 1941 produced three models; an advanced trainer, an operational trainer for air crew training which included gun turrets, and a transport model as shown here at Chofu in September 1945. Its bright green against a light grey produced a colourful image. Note the detail in the tail insignia. *(J Gallagher)*

Allied pilots were very impressed with the performance of the Ki-84 "Frank". When engaged in combat, the "Frank" was every bit a match for Allied aircraft. One or more captured K-48s were flight-tested by TAIU pilots at Clark AB, helping to develop better ways in which to engage the "Frank" in combat. This fighter was powered by a 2,200 hp engine, yet only weighed 4,387 lb when empty. *(J Gallagher)*

The most exciting aircraft seen at Chofu Air Base was the one and only Nakajima Ki-87. This was a very large aircraft when compared to those at its side of more conventional size. The design of this aircraft began in November 1942 with intended completion date of three prototypes by January 1945. The first flight test of the Ki-87 was made in April 1945.

*(J Gallagher)*

What was most impressive about this aircraft was the turbo supercharger which was a rarity on Japanese aircraft. This occupied a substantial part of the right side of the nose, being part of the Nakajima Ha-44 eighteen-cylinder engine, rated at 2,400 hp at take-off. It was estimated that it would give this aircraft a top speed of 378 knots at 36,000 feet, a significant advantage over the then contemporary fighters.

*(J Gallagher)*

The success of this Nakajima Ki-87 interceptor fighter was predicated on perfecting its turbo-supercharged engine. Engineering development of this type was conducted at Nakajima's Mitaka Engine Research Works on the west edge of Tokyo which used this nearby Chofu Airfield. This one-and-only Ki-87 was set aside at Chofu along with the Ki-100 and Ki-115 for evaluation by the Allies.

*(J Gallagher)*

Another view of the same Ki-100 reveals the very worn tail insignia of the 244th Fighter Sentai to which the Ki-61 "Tonys" pictured were also assigned. It had a very time-worn olive drab finish which lacked any lustre as did its grey under-surfaces. The Hinomaru, instead of blood red, was weathered into almost pink. This aircraft had far more appealing lines when seen with a propeller that has a very large streamlined propeller-spinner. *(J Gallagher)*

Showa airfield was situated a few miles west of Tachikawa and mostly served the Showa Airplane Co. Its main product was the licenced manufacturing of the Douglas DC-3 that served as a Navy transport. One can be seen in the background in a semi completed state in this factory building at Showa. The American is inspecting the propeller of the Kawasaki N1K2-J "George" fighter. It is an aircraft that was to be produced by Showa until interrupted by the end of the war. *(SC 215570)*

***Showa Air Base:*** To the immediate west of Tachikawa was Showa airfield. This was the location of the Showa Aeroplane Company, which from early 1945 was owned by the Mitsui Bassan Kaisha K.K., one of Japan's largest industrial companies. It was here that Showa established the licence production of the Douglas DC-3 for the Imperial Japanese Navy. By the end of the war it was entering production of the Kawanishi N1K2-J "George" fighter, and Nakajima Ki-115 Tsurugi special attack plane.

In the early Occupation, the manufacturing buildings were converted for rebuilding US military vehicles for extended service, giving employment to many Japanese. The airfield proper, which was under the north-bound landing flight path to the heavy traffic at Yokota Air Base, was turned into one of the better golf courses in Japan for US Occupational Forces recreational purposes.

*Yokota Air Base:* Also known as Fussa Air Base during its wartime period because of its adjacency to that village, Yokota became, and still is the US military aviation hub in Japan. As an Imperial Japanese Army installation, it became operational in 1940 having as its first unit, the Army Flight Experiment Department (Rikugun Hiko Jikken Bu). It was an organization developed from air technological units located at nearby Tachikawa Air Base. In late 1942, considerable reorganization in air matériel functions at Tachikawa caused many activities to be expanded and shifted to nearby Fussa Airfield. The base then became the Army Air Evaluation Department (Rikugun Koku Shinsa Bu) and absorbed part of the Army Aviation Technical Research Department also from Tachikawa. These changes made Fussa the centre of all Army flight testing, affording unrestricted field boundaries from which to operate higher performance aircraft.

In the field of cast-off production DC-3s at Showa was this one evidence of a wooden DC-3 version at Showa. Before the discovery of this photograph, the Japanese "Wooden Gooney" was treated as a rumour. It was to be produced in non-strategic wood in the interest of conserving critical materials. The wing protruding into its side is that of an Aichi D3A2 "Val", an earlier type produced at Showa. *(Geo. Johnson)*

Yokota Air Base, also referred to as Fussa Air Base in the early days, had a wealth of Army aircraft of different types on its airfield during the early days of the Occupation. Few photographs seem to have been taken there by Occupation personnel. This enlarged photo of the south-west corner of the field that was taken 28 August 1945 attests to this quantity. Nearly every type of Army operational aircraft can be identified in this photograph. Base operations is on the field-side of the circle driveway.

*(USAAF 6th Recon Group)*

There is no record of actual combat air units specifically being assigned at Fussa Air Base. However, many aircraft on various combat missions utilized this field. In 1944, when air raids became a threat to Japan, aircraft of the Evaluation Department and Maintenance Division were armed, and frequently engaged American aircraft. In this combat role they came under the operational control of the 10th Air Division which was responsible for the Kanto Air Defense Sector.

Under American occupancy, Fussa, now Yokota Air Base, became an ever-growing installation. The first American unit to occupy the base was a vanguard of the 2nd Combat Cargo Group. While Yokota's facilities had been adequate for Japanese aircraft, the runway soon cracked under the strain of that unit's heavily-laden C-46 cargo aircraft. A grass strip was used for take-offs and landings until fall rains forced all flying to cease in December 1945 when the 2nd Cargo Group moved to Atsugi. Major rehabilitating took place that winter to prepare for the arrival of the 3rd Bombardment Group with its three squadrons of Douglas A-20 Havocs and A-26 Invaders. During the Korean War, the FEAF Bomber Command took up station at Yokota, along with Headquarters for the 92nd and 98th Bombardment Wings and their B-29s. The 35th Fighter Wing was also an important and early tenant at Yokota AB.

One major surprise found at Yokota was this P-40 parked beside Base Operations. The tail insignia shows that of the Akeno Fighter School where it would have served as a training aid for filming or simulated air engagements.
*(W Shaw)*

Yokota Base Operations as it appeared in 1992 while using the P-40 photograph for perspective. Little exterior change has been made since.
*(R Mikesh)*

This is the only known photograph of the one Tachikawa SS-1 experimental aircraft. It was taken at Yokota Air Base when Americans first arrived. Engineless in this picture, this was a test aircraft having a pressurized cabin very much like that of the USAAF Lockheed XC-35 built for the same kind of testing in 1937. Both used Lockheed components with an all new circular fuselage for each. The USAAF basic structure was a Lockheed 10, while Tachikawa used licence-built Lockheed 14 wings and tail. The Japanese programme was started in 1940, four years after the American project was conceived.

Two very contrasting photographs of Yokota AB show changes made during the first 28 years following the end of the Pacific War. The photograph at the left shows the configuration of Yokota on 28 August 1945, the day the first Americans arrived at Atsugi AB to the south. An enlarged view from this picture of the aircraft parking area at the south west corner of the field is shown on page 85. Its hard surface runway was a short 4,000 ft. Today it stretches to 12,000 feet with overruns. The boot-shaped area in the picture to the east was formerly a bomb dump and aircraft dispersal area for the Japanese. Today it serves as a military dependent housing area – see 1 in photograph opposite.

The area west of Tokyo shown in the photo at the right was once a major hub of Japanese Army testing of aircraft and manufacture. Today, it is heavily dominated with aviation activity and manufacturing. In the centre of this view taken in 1973 is Yokota Air Base (1), once the flight test base for the Army Air Evaluation Department (Rikugun Koku Shinsa Bu). To its south east was the Showa Aircraft Company (2) which is now a truck body plant adjacent to the Shown Golf Course in the former airfield area. To the east is Tachikawa AB (3) from which much of the flight testing activities were initiated during the war in conjunction with nearby Yokota AB. To the north is the modern test track and manufacturing of Nissan automobiles (4). On the north edge of Yokota AB is the Ishikawajima aircraft jet-engine plant (5).

**Irumagawa Air Base:** A straight line seven miles to the north-east of Yokota lay Irumagawa Air Base, acquiring its name from the adjacent town and river. This was the air academy for the Imperial Japanese Army Air Force which was constructed in 1937. The product here was considered to be the nucleus of regular officers whose early military training often started at the age of thirteen to fifteen years. Since the academy side of the base was located near the town of Toyooka, it quite naturally acquired the popular name of "Toyooka Shikan Gakko"—the last two words meaning "officer school". (Some references are made to Toyooka Airfield, but this was an auxiliary to the base, mid-way between Fussa and Irumagawa, more properly known as Sakato airfield.) Flying activities were primarily that of orange-painted Tachikawa Type 95 biplane trainers for aviation cadet training.

To the amazement of the first Americans to arrive on the base, they found a full size facsimile of a B-29 Super Fortress in an open area of the base. Not until recent years was it learned that this was used for training suicide teams on how to set explosives to destroy B-29s while parked on the ground. Teams were to be carried at night by air to American B-29 bases on Guam and Tinian. The war ended before this was implemented.

From the unmarked roads, this was a difficult base to locate from the existing road system that seemingly did not lead directly to the base. Through some unexplained means, one of the "Baka Bombs" found at Atsugi, made its way to the turning point outside the base to become an unmistakable marker for the entrance access road. In time this "Baka Bomb" became a symbol for the base and it was later more properly displayed in front of the headquarters building for many years until returned to the Japanese in the 1960s.

Under American occupancy, this became known as Johnson Air Base in memory of Colonel Gerald A Johnson, the past commander of the 49th Fighter Group of P-38s. This was the top fighter unit in the Pacific War with more confirmed air victories (677) than any other group. Johnson, after accumulating 22 victories for himself, was killed in a post-war B-25 over Tokyo Bay on 7 October 1945. This base became home for many USAF units over the years, beginning with Headquarters for the 5th Air Force, and later the 41st Air Division. Flying units began with the 8th Photo Reconnaissance Squadron, 35th Fighter group, and 3rd Bombardment Wing, to name a few. When the flying facility of the base was transferred to the Japanese Air Self Defense Force in early 1960s, the remainder of the base became the Johnson Family Housing Annex to supplement Yokota Air Base facilities. By the end of the 1960s, the base was entirely returned to Japanese control as Iruma Air Base.

Irumagawa Air Base was another field visited by Americans that held aircraft of interest. In this case, neighbouring youngsters from outside the base that heretofore had been off limits to them, find this Mitsubishi Ki-67, code named "Peggy", of great fascination as they swarm over the fuselage. This was an aircraft of the 14th Hiko Sentai, a kamikaze-type unit, stripped of all armament and made into a "flying bomb". Note unusual object in nose section that may be part of its destructive force. *(J Gallagher)*

This angle of the same "Peggy" shows that the defensive armament has been removed or faired over which would support the planning thought of a one-time crash-dive flight mission. The red tail markings identify this aircraft belonging to the 2nd Chutai, 14th Sentai. Aircraft was overall brown, with grey bottom. *(J Gallagher)*

Another "Peggy", in a bullet and rocket damaged hangar at Irumagawa AB, is unflyable because of having holes in its fabric covered elevators and is missing the left wing tip. This was a modern aircraft by World War II standards, one particularly blessed with a remarkably high speed. Army tests were so successful as a torpedo bomber, that the Navy took deliveries of these aircraft as well, and known to them as Yasukuni. *(J Gallagher)*

The design and capability of the Ki-67 Hiryu, the Japanese name for what the Allies called "Peggy", was so advanced that plans were made for several combat versions. Besides being a high performance bomber and torpedo aircraft, others included modifications for carrying a 75 mm anti-aircraft cannon for attacks against B-29s while staying out of counter machine-gun fire. Not appearing in the war until October 1944, had it been advanced by one more year, the Allies would have seen "Peggy" in many forms and in greater numbers. *(J Gallagher)*

This is a Kawasaki Ki-48 "Lily", a type that was also set aside for the final defence against the assault landings upon Japan. These were slow, light bombers, but did their share of the support bombing for the Japanese Army throughout their areas in which the Army was engaged.

*(J Gallagher)*

Of all the night fighters seen at Atsugi and defensive fighters seen elsewhere, this Kawasaki Ki-48 "Lily" was the only aircraft that photographer Jim Gallagher found that was painted an overall black. Its purpose is unknown since its black colouring was not considered a worthy one for painting other aircraft like this one. *(J Gallagher)*

These few aircraft found at Irumagawa AB were grouped in one area of the base when photographed in October 1945. Since a grouping such as this was not visible in the surveillance photograph taken on 28 August 1945, these aircraft are presumed to have been those seen dispersed and brought back to the airfield after that date. This Ki-46 "Dinah" is but a shell of being operational. All the glass panels are missing as is the fuselage top that covers the main fuel tank. *(J Gallagher)*

Surprisingly, these Mitsubishi Ki-30 light bombers, code named "Ann", were still in the Japanese inventory despite their obsolescence. These found at Irumagawa AB had their wings removed and were being used as maintenance trainers. Roughly a dozen or more were on the base. The tail insignia is that of the Toyooka Shikan Gako, or Toyooka (nearby town) Officers School. *(J Gallagher)*

Left: A close look reveals that this is a well constructed mock-up of a B-29 complete with American national insignia 89 Irumagawa air base. The photograph above reveals its position. The mock-up was created as a training aid. Near the end of the war suicide teams were being trained as to how best to place destructive charges in B-29s following a massive one way night air assault on the airfield Guam Tinian. Their plan was to destroy as many B-29s on the ground as possible before being apprehended.

***Tokorozawa Air Base:*** Four-and-a-half miles south-east of Johnson AB, in the direction of Tokyo, was Tokorozawa Air Base on the north side of the city by that name. This had been the home base for the 27th Sentai, equipped with interceptor configured Ki-45kai "Nicks". Remnants of their earlier Ki-32 "Marys" and Ki 51b "Sonias" were present around the airfield. Of greatest interest to the Occupation Forces were the sleek lines of the Ki-84 "Franks" belonging to the 200th Sentai assigned there.

This former military airfield became the US Army Logistic Depot Tokorozawa, its former flying field acreage being filled with row upon row of US military vehicles, weaponry, and crated goods of all kinds. This was a major arsenal for collecting equipment following the Pacific War, and seeing to their reconditioning. This readiness was fortunate since the Korean War soon followed. After that war, it again became a collecting point for these munitions until eventually phased out and returned to Japanese control.

***Narimasu Air Base:*** Another flying facility that was not utilized as such by the Occupation Forces was Narimasu Air Base. This was situated on the north-west edge of Tokyo and played an important part in the defence of that city and targets further inland. Two fighter units are known to have been stationed there, the 47th Sentai flying Nakajima Ki-84 "Franks" that when moved at the turn of 1944/45 was replaced by the 70 Sentai flying Nakajima Ki-44 "Tojos" that operated there until the end of the war.

Narimasu was another airfield that Occupation Forces found little use for once the Japanese aircraft were disposed of. In order to house the ever-growing population of American servicemen and their dependents, this former Imperial Japanese Army Air Force base became Grant Heights Family Housing Annex to support surrounding military facilities. Grotto-like hardened hangars were still apparent through the 1960s, and the unmistakable runway provided a remarkably wide tree-lined street for one of the avenues of dependent houses.

Narimasu airfield was another Army air defence base for the Tokyo area. It was situated on the north-west corner of Tokyo in close proximity to the vital engine plant of Nakajima at Musashi. When these pictures were taken seven months before the Occupation Forces entered the base, these young Japanese pilots were flying Nakajima Ki-44 Shoki fighters against the onslaught of US Navy air attacks and night bombing of Tokyo by B-29s.

*(S Hayashi)*

A cold day at Narimasu airfield is in evidence by the skiff of snow over the field and the covers for the engines of these Nakajima Ki-44 Shoki fighters. One of the early residents of this field by Occupation Forces was the TAIU team that was charged with the collection of Japanese aircraft from all the corners of the Japanese home islands. Strangely, the Ki-44s gathered for shipment to the United States were obtained from Kashiwa airfield, north-east of Tokyo. *(S Hayashi)*

***Haneda Airport:*** During the war, this commercial airport was used militarily in the air defence of Tokyo. At the end of hostilities, the American forces used it primarily as their Air Transport Command base for all overseas flights in and out of Japan, along with commercial carriers. As Japan returned more to normality in post Occupation years, this military activity was transferred to Tachikawa AB, and Haneda became a Japanese-operated commercial international airport once again.

***Oppama Naval Air Station:*** Located adjacent to the Yokosuka Naval Facility south of Yokohama on Tokyo Bay, this airfield was more often referred to as Yokosuka Naval Air Base. Oppama was the focal point for nearly all Naval aircraft under development because this activity was the responsibility of the Kaigun Koku-Gijutsu-Sho (Naval Technical Air Arsenal) that was located there, and better known by its acronym *Kugisho*. This was a field with short runways and hazardous approaches from the west. As Naval aircraft increased in their flight performance, flight testing was gradually moved to larger facilities such as Misawa AB in Northern Honshu and Kisarazu AB on the other side of Tokyo Bay.

The US Navy and Marines used the Yokosuka facilities as part of their initial move in the Occupation. The Oppama Airfield became the focal point for the gathering of Japanese aircraft for their move by ship to the United States, but air operations were most likely ended around the early part of 1946 after a few months of Occupational Forces service. It remained operational as a seaplane base well into the 1950s but with limited activity. With the phase-out of flying boat operations within the US Navy, so went the Oppama facility as a flight station.

In the final chaotic days of the war, any airfield was looked upon as a suitable safe haven for the returning Japanese air warriors, regardless of their branch of service or unit location if home base was not in easy reach. For this reason, it was not surprising to find a mix of many types of aircraft at any one of these bases. Until their complete destruction, these Japanese warbirds provided interest and sources for souvenirs for many of the Occupation Force personnel that found these enemy aircraft fascinating and unusual. As more US Forces occupied these bases, space became a greater premium and complete aircraft were soon moved to the scrap heaps. When these aircraft were ignominiously stacked helter-skelter in scrap piles, they lost their identity and dignity. As one of the aircraft seekers recalls: "while clambering over these remains, one got the feeling that this was no different or more glamorous than climbing through an automobile junk yard. You forgot that these had been the feared weapons of war for a forceful and bitter enemy just a few weeks before."

Tokyo's Haneda Airport was a relatively small airfield at the time this picture was taken one year after the Pacific War ended. With very little civil aviation during the war, it primarily served military needs. Post-war commercial demands upon Haneda expanded this man-made island in all directions into Tokyo Bay, eventually outgrowing itself to where it is no longer the hub of Japan's commercial air traffic.

*(SC 249667)*

Oppama Airfield was a significant facility to the Japanese Navy that supported the many Naval activities at nearby Yokosuka. The important shipyard area begins at the bottom of this picture. This airfield was the gathering point for the hundred or so aircraft to be sent by ship to the United States. Soon into the Occupation of Japan, this airfield was closed except for its seaplane operations. The Navy moved its land plane functions to Atsugi Air Base, and Oppama airfield was quickly forgotten.

Technical Air Intelligence Unit teams used a number of types of aircraft in the Japanese aircraft retrieval process. This Grumman TBF Avenger, "Navy 595", assigned to the TAIU team based at Narimasu, is seen here being refuelled at Tachikawa Air Base.

*(T Brundridge via Air Force Museum)*

This anti-submarine patrol aircraft "Lorna" heads towards Oppama Air Base near Yokosuka, monitored by a US Navy Corsair. This escort was to assure that the Japanese pilots took no offensive action during these flights. These precautions were soon discontinued. *(USMC 140521)*

# CHAPTER V
# GATHERING THE BEST

## The Spoils of War

In the final stages of the war, the Japanese Army and Navy kept their aircraft on the ground, hidden beneath camouflage, in underground hangars and scattered over dispersal areas as far as five miles from airfields. In the air they had been overwhelmed by Allied airpower and rendered impotent. On the ground, they were able to be saved for the final and desperate suicidal attempt at repelling the landing forces as Japan was sure to be invaded by the enemy. Beyond all doubt, these aircraft were the most lethal threat still in the hands and under the control of Japan, a country extremely embittered by certain defeat. Such an attack would not have changed the final verdict of the war, but it could have served as satisfying revenge for the dying warrior clans.

As surrender negotiations were unfolding, and as a counter-measure to this possible last ditch air threat, Japan was issued instructions to expose to aerial surveillance, all aircraft otherwise concealed. Periodically, photo-reconnaissance flights were made over the Japanese airfields, whereby an accounting could be made of remaining aircraft. Any unauthorised aircraft movement on the ground that might indicate grouping for an attack was carefully checked by these photographs. Even one incident at this delicate juncture in stabilizing a peace, would impart more stringent restrictions on Japan by the Occupation Forces.

One of the stipulations made to the Japanese in preparing selected aircraft for ferry flights was that they be re-marked with the US National insignia. This Japanese Navy Kyushu Q1W1 Tokai, code named "Lorna" stands in readiness at an airfield near Fukuoka on Kyushu.

*(USMC 140520)*

With the arrival of the Occupation Forces came the Technical Air Intelligence Units to search Japan for technologically significant objects. The TAIU established their base of operations at Narimasu, which was situated at the northwest edge of Tokyo. From this airfield, up until this time, Nakajima Ki-44 "Tojos" of the 70th Fighter Group had desperately waged a losing effort to defend the city from attacks by B-29s.

To provide the most rapid and practical means for members of the TAIU to inspect the many Japanese airfields, the unit had three Grumman TBM Avengers assigned to them. Although TAIU teams were made up of Army, Navy and RAF members, it was not uncommon for Army pilots to fly these Avengers to these various airfields for inspection trips. One Corsair pilot, while patrolling over Japan, joined up smartly on the wing of one of these lumbering Avengers. His relaxed expression quickly changed to complete bewilderment when he recognized the Army uniforms on the crewmen of this Navy aircraft. The Army pilot, not wishing to pass up a golden opportunity in this unusual situation, raised the microphone to his mouth and with great deliberation announced smugly: "We stole it!"

During these early days of the Occupation, TAIU teams departed their base at Narimasu airfield first thing in the morning and flew to pre-planned inspections of outlying airfields. After an aerial survey of the area, the pilot would land the Avenger and its team of one officer, one translator/interpreter, and one photographer who would look over the local Japanese aircraft and other equipment for any unusual technology. Also being sought were the best flying examples of new aircraft. In time, those selected would be flown to Yokosuka, a gathering point for shipment to the United States. Once these items, mostly aircraft, were located and identified, guards were posted to ensure they remained safe until such time they could be flown away.

Long shadows reveal the early hour that these "George" fighters were warmed up and ready for the ferry flight to Yokosuka. The largest quantity of serviceable "George" fighters were found at the Naval Base at Omura in western Kyushu. This type Japanese Navy fighter was one of the latest to confront the advancing Allied Forces.
*(USMC 137786)*

Teams of the TAIUs covered seaplane bases as well. This "Jake" appears to be in complete and in serviceable condition sans propeller and beaching gear. Tail markings show it to belong to the 901st Kokutai that was responsible for coastal patrol. *(SC 290571)*

Of the many ferry flights that were required to move nearly a hundred aircraft, all were flown by Japanese pilots. From the beginning, as part of the surrender terms, the safe movement of equipment was a responsibility mandated to the Japanese military. The co-operation given by the Japanese to the Americans was reflected by unquestioning obedience in compliance with their Emperor's wishes. The Japanese military forces, although in the process of being systematically demobilized, were still a functioning organization and managed most of the details in preparing the selected aircraft for flight to the collecting point at Oppama Air Base, Yokosuka. Some eager American pilots tried very hard to be included among those ferrying these Japanese aircraft, but since the responsibility for safety and the effective movement of these aircraft was that of the Japanese military, Japanese officers insisted that only their own experienced pilots fly the aircraft until the delivery was completed.

Procedures for these ferry missions that took place on previously arranged dates called for the TAIU team members to fly to the departure base in their TBM early in the morning of that day. This contingent functioned as the co-ordinating body and control tower for the departure. When the pre-arranged fighter escort arrived overhead, this signalled that it was clear for the Japanese aircraft to take off. After becoming airborne, they were to remain in the airfield flight pattern and make two practice approaches to the runway. If everything functioned properly, the aircraft would proceed on a direct route to Yokosuka with the Avenger containing the TAIU team leading the way. In the event that a Japanese aircraft experienced any mechanical difficulty that would prevent it from safely making the flight, it would land and an alternate aircraft with crew already standing by would take its place.

This trio of Mitsubishi F1M2 "Pete" Observation Seaplanes await the word concerning their destruction. These were located at Sasabo Naval Base in western Kyushu. They belonged to the 951st Kokutai
*(USMC 136984)*

Upon reaching the Oppama Airfield, at Yokosuka, the TBM pilot would make contact with the tower to announce the arrival of the Japanese aircraft. The Avenger would land, leading the Japanese aircraft, and when all was secured, the escorting fighters would proceed back to their home base.

This type of operation worked well until one day the escorting fighters did not show up. The story of this incident is remembered well by Theodore T Brundage, who was an Army Air Corps Captain at the time and in charge of the gathering of many of these aircraft. Ted Brundage had joined the TAIU (SWPA) at Clark in May 1945 as the unit commander and moved with them to Japan. On this occasion, Brundage was supervising the movement of three Kawanishi "George 21" fighters along with one ground spare from Himeji Airfield in central Honshu.

"We waited and waited for the P-38s to show up," he recalls, "but nothing happened. As the day progressed, we had to do something. Since the Japanese had been co-operating fully in all these operations, we decided to make the flight without the fighter escort. Just to make sure that the Japanese understood who was in charge, we rotated the gun turret on our Avenger while we were preparing to take-off, just to make this point clear. Thinking back now, the Japanese must have thought this to be a feeble and needless act to flex this single .50 calibre machine-gun as a threat to these fast and nimble fighters. On the other hand, we Americans were in a strange country, in the midst of our former enemy, and had cause to be a bit apprehensive as to what might happen. The flight went very well, and from then on we dispensed with having fighter escort for these ferry flights, which solved much of the co-ordination effort."

After saying this, Brundage recalled one incident that was an exception. In a similar situation soon after removing the need for fighter escort, another set of Japanese fighters from another air base got airborne according to the planned flight to Oppama. By the time the Avenger with its TAIU team on board got into the air, the Japanese fighters were nowhere to be seen. The sky was frantically searched for these aircraft, but they did not reappear. There was nothing to do but for the Avenger crew to proceed according to the plan to Oppama and face the consequences upon arrival.

As the TBM neared the traffic pattern at Oppama, out of nowhere, the flight of Japanese fighters popped up from below on to the Avenger's wing in tight formation as if this were routine! At least the mission ended as it should, for the fighters smartly peeled off and proceeded to land, followed by the Avenger whose crew made no mention of the incident. As with all other ferry flight terminations, the Japanese turned in their flying equipment to the Americans, and were escorted to the gate of the base. It was up to them to find their way back to their home base.

According to a news clipping account taken from a November 1945 edition of the *Stars and Stripes,* the armed forces overseas newspaper, "there were three aircraft lost in the entire operation that were due to accidents. One accident involved a Japanese aircraft and a Navy Corsair, but it was a taxiing mishap of minor importance."

The gathering point at Oppama was a bustle of activity for the weeks that this collecting was taking place. As the inventory increased, so did the need for surface craft for moving these aircraft to the United States. It was a confusing time, and little information about this movement has been made in official correspondence.

This Aichi B7A2 Navy Carrier Attack Bomber, "Grace", was a late comer to the war. Only 114 were built to serve as torpedo and level bombers for carriers that no longer existed. Americans push this "Grace" of the 752nd Kokutai out of the hangar for closer inspection and possible shipment to the US.

*(80-G-344083)*

Many locations visited by the inspecting TAIU teams found order as shown here as an expression of Japanese co-operation with American Occupation Forces. This shows a hangar at Omura Naval Air Base on Kyushu with demilitarized Kawanishi N1K2-J "George" fighters. *(USMC 147335)*

This Kawanishi H6K5 "Mavis" flying-boat was found by a TAIU team at Takuma Seaplane Base on Shikoku Island. This 1936 vintage patrol bomber and transport was considered too outdated to warrant evaluation. Accordingly, all of this type were soon destroyed. The Kawanishi H8K2 "Emily" was a far better choice for evaluation. *(SC 225871)*

When the Occupation Forces reached Otsu Air Base on Lake Biwa north of Kyoto, they found these trainer seaplanes, code named "Willow", disassembled and stacked like cord wood in compliance with making all aircraft unairworthy. The larger "Jake" reconnaissance seaplanes had been scuttled by puncturing their floats. (SC 218696)

When TAIU teams visited the Nakajima Aircraft Company at Ohta, they discovered for the first time, the existence of Japanese jet aircraft. This is the Nakajima Kikka, one of twenty-five preproduction aircraft on the assembly line. Two others had been completed and one had flown just before the war end.

This Tachikawa Ki-74 was a very advanced bomber for its time period. Designed with exceptional long range, it was to be capable of bombing the United States from Japan's most forward bases in the Pacific. Engine problems curtailed development and thus were never used in combat. This view of Japanese preparing what was known as "Patsy", was probably taken at Yokota or Tachikawa Air Bases.

Another advanced aircraft of the Japanese was this Mitsubishi Ki-46-IV "Dinah", one of three aircraft saved at Yokota AB for flight evaluation. This picture taken on October 29, 1945 was taken just prior to the aircraft's ferry flight from Yokota to Oppama. Shown here is the Japanese pilot (right), Major Katsukura, along with Major Piper, who was in charge of the transfer of the "Dinah". Painted on the nose is "Sayonara Trophy".

The Ki-77 rests at Oppama Air Base as it is being readied with a protective black coating for the shipment to the United States. This airplane was intended to make a non-stop good-will flight from Tokyo to New York in 1940 but the deteriorating international situation prevented this from happening. It later proved its endurance for such a flight over a closed course in Manchuria in July 1944.

The gathering of these aircraft at Oppama Air Base was a collection of many types when being prepared for shipment to the United States. The most rare of the types shown in this picture are the single and the two-seat versions of the Nakajima J5N1 Tenrai in the back row, right. "Irvings", "Bettys", "Judys" and one "Myrt" are the bulk of what is shown here.

In the years following this mustering of Japanese aircraft, a committee of Japanese historians, and several independent American historians, particularly this author, have made attempts at locating or reconstructing an inventory of the aircraft that were shipped from Japan. Lists were found that showed which aircraft were desired for shipment, while other lists were estimates from Japanese sources. The Air Matériel Command issued a Catalogue of Foreign Equipment that was dated 10 March, 1946. It listed only those Japanese aircraft that could be made available for selected industrial study and could have not listed some that were shipped. Unfortunately, none of these could be considered an accurate inventory that reflected all the aircraft actually sent to the United States.

The commander of the TAI Unit in Japan, Ted Brundage, retained in his collection of wartime memorabilia, a listing of these aircraft which must be the most reliable of all. Brundage was responsible for the loading phase of these aircraft, and had retained the original treasure-trove document along with photographs. This time-stained document was on the typical Japanese tissue writing paper, prepared primarily in English with pencil writing by a Japanese who at times, in desperation for the proper English word, had to resort to writing it in Japanese. Not only did these inventories show the airfields from which most of these aircraft had come, but some serial numbers were also included.

SCHEDULE FOR PREPARATION OF JAPANESE ARMY AIRCRAFT
FOR DELIVERY TO THE U.S. AIR FORCES FOR FLIGHT TEST

(Second Revised Plan)

8 October 1945
Further revised to 11 October 1945

| Type | Number Required | Avail- able | Airfield (Responsible Depot) | Condition for delivery | Remarks |
|---|---|---|---|---|---|
| Ki-21-II [Sally] | 2 | *** 2 [0] | Yokota & Tokorozawa | | [Doubtful if shipped.] |
| Ki-44-II [Tojo] | 4 | 4 | Kashiwa (Tachikawa M.A.F.) [*2] | Flyable | 2 are ready. 2 will be ready 10 Oct. |
| Ki-45 [Nick] | 2 | 2 | Shiroi or Fujigaya | Flyable | Ready. |
| Ki-46-III [Dinah] | 4 | 4 | Kodama (1st Air Army) [Koku Gun] | Flyable | 2 are ready, Nos. 5444 & 5453 2 will be ready 15 Oct., Nos. 8053 & 8058. |

| | | | | | |
|---|---|---|---|---|---|
| Ki-46-IV [Dinah] | 4 | 2 2 | Yokota Mibu (Test Bureau) [*3] | Crated for shipment. | Nos. 5004 & 5006. Nos. 5007 & 5008. Still under development. |
| Ki-48-II [Lily] | 4 | 4 | Nasuno (1st Air Army) [Koku Gun] | Flyable | Ready, Nos. 1158, 1216, 1089, 1082, and 2027. |
| Ki-49-II [Helen] | 4 | 4 | Toyama (Training Air Division) | Flyable | Ready about 15 Oct. |
| Ki-61-II [Tony] | 4 | 4 | Itami (Osaka M.A.F.) [*2] | Flyable | Ready about 10 Oct. |
| Ki-67 [Peggy] | 4 | 4 | Kameyama [*1] (Kagamigahara M.A.F.) [*2] | Flyable | 1 is ready. 3 will be ready about 15 Oct. |
| Ki-70 * [Clara] | 3 | 1 | Tachikawa Factory | Crated for shipment | |
| Ki-74 [Patsy] | 4 | 2 | Yokota (Test Bureau) [*3] | Flyable | Ready about 20 Oct. |
| | | 2 | Tachikawa Factory | Condition unknown | Not yet delivered to the Army. |
| Ki-77 * [A-26] | 1 | 1 | Kofu | Crated for shipment ** | Not yet delivered to the Army. |
| Ki-83 | 1 | 1 | Matsumoto | | |
| Ki-84 [Frank] | 2 | 4 | Utsunomiya South (Utsunomiya M.A.F.) [*2] | Flyable | Ready. [108, 119] |
| Ki-87 * | 1 | 1 | Chofu (Nakajima Factory) | Crated for shipment | Not yet delivered to the Army. |
| Ki-93 * | 1 | 1 | Takahagi (Kofu-Kosho) | Crated for shipment | Nearing completion. |
| Ki-94 * | 1 | [1] | | | Not in inventory. |

| | | | | | |
|---|---|---|---|---|---|
| Ki-100 [Tony] | 4 | 6 [4] | Komaki (Kagamihara M.A.F.) [*2] | Flyable | 4 are ready. |
| Ki-100-II * [Tony] | 4 | 1 | Komaki (Kagamihara M.A.F.) [*2] | Crated for shipment | Not yet delivered to the Army. |
| Ki-102-A [Randy] | 4 | 2 [4] | Togane (lst Air Army) | Crated for shipment. | Few in use, but none flyable now. |
| Ki-102-B [Randy] | 4 | 1 | Akashi | Flyable | Ready about 10 Oct. |
| | | 3 | Osaka E. (Osaka M.A.F.) [*2] | Flyable | |
| Ki-105 * [Buzzard] | 2 | 2 | Kyoto (Kokusai Factory) | Condition unknown | If not flyable, would be too unwieldy to crate. |
| Ki-106 * [Frank] | 4 | 4 | Tachikawa (Tachikawa Factory) | At factory for repairs. | None delivered to the Army. |
| Ki-109 [Peggy] | 4 | 2 | Nitta (or Kiryu) (1st Air Army) [Koku Gun] | Flyable | Ready about 10 Oct. Nos. 10 & 11. |
| Ki-115 * | 4 | 4 | Ohta (Nakajima Factory) | To be shipped by truck. | None delivered to the Army. Flight considered dangerous. |

Total: 67 [69] Army aircraft

Note: Aircraft that are marked with an asterisk (*) indicate that these are test aircraft for the manufacturer, and their present conditions, and availability for delivery are now under inquiry through the Ministry of Commerce & Industry, which has taken over the responsibility of the former Ministry for Supply.

[Note: Information within brackets [ ] is author added information.]
[** at Ki-77: Probable error. Photos show ferry flight and protective coating for deck shipment.]

[*** : Another original document, undated, gives these quantity figures, in brackets, which differ from the document reproduced here.]

[*1] :   Kameyama, in Chiba Prefecture, was the town near Kitaise Airfield, which may be the more correct name.  Locally referred to as Kasado Airfield.

[*2] :   Military Air Field

[*3] :   Test Bureau is the *Rikugun Koku Shinsa-bu* or Department of Army Air Evaluation located at Fussa (Yokota) AB.

## LIST OF AIRCRAFT REQUIRED FROM JAPANESE NAVY AIR FORCE
### (Undated)

| Type | Number Required | Avail- able | Airfield | Serial No. | Remarks |
|---|---|---|---|---|---|
| A6M6 Reisen 62 (Zeke) | 4 | 4 | Yatabe | | |
| A6M8 Reisen 64 (Zeke) | 4 | 1 | Misawa | [14] | (None completed. Possibly A6M8c.) |
| A7M2 Reppu (Sam) | 4 | 2 | Matsumoto | | Move by train. |
| B6N2 Tensan 12 (Jill) | 4 | ***<br>4 [2] | Suzuka | | |
| B6N3 Tenzan 13 (Jill) | 1 | 1 | Yokosuka | | Original document showed B7N2, but Tenzan 13 is B6N3. |
| B7A1 Ryusei (Grace) | 4 | 3 [4] | Yokosuka | 317, 812 and 921 | |
| C6N1 Saiun 11 (Myrt) | 4 | 2<br>2 | Yokosuka<br>Kisarazu | 735, 4161 | |
| C6N2 Saiun 12 (Myrt) | 4 | 1 | Misawa | | |
| D4Y2 Suisei 12 (Judy) | 4 | 4 [2] | Yokosuka | | |
| D4Y3 Suisei 33 (Judy) | 3 | 2<br>1 | Yokosuka<br>Nagoya (Ibo) | 1620, 1959 [22] | |

| | | | | | |
|---|---|---|---|---|---|
| D4Y4 Suisei 43 (Judy) | 4 | 4 | Nagoya (Ibo) | [26, 43] | |
| E16A1 Zuiun (Paul) | 4 | 1 [3] | Sasebo Tsuchiura | [70] | 2 available but not flyable. |
| G4M3 Mod.34 (Betty) | 4 | 1 1 | Matsushima Yokosuka | 3006 | |
| H8K3 Mod.12 (Emily) | 1 | 1 | Yokohama | | |
| J1N1 Gekko (Irving) | 4 | 1 3 [1] | Yokosuka Atsugi | 7334 | |
| J2M3 Raiden 31 (Jack) | 4 | 1 [0] 3 | Suzuka Atsugi | | |
| J2M5 Raiden 33 (Jack) | 4 | 4 [1] | Atsugi | | |
| J5N1 Tenrai | 4 | 2 | Yokosuka | 11, 16 | Only 2 available |
| M6A1 Seiran | 4 | 1 1 | Yokosuka Fukuyama | [47] | |
| N1K1 Kyofu (Rex) | 4 | 4 | Kowa | [40, 47] | |
| N1K1-J Shiden 11 (George) | 3 | 3 [2] | Himeji | [41] | |
| N1K2-J Shiden 21 (George) | 4 | 2 2 | Yokosuka Omura | 71, 533 | 1 Exp. at Showa and Kisarazu. |
| P1Y1 Ginga (Frances) | 4 | 2 2 | Yokosuka Matsushima | | |
| Q1W1 Tokai (Lorna) | 4 | 2 2 | Yokosuka Hakata | 37, 170 | |
| R2Y1 Keiun | 1 | 1 [0] | Yokosuka [Kasarazu] | | |

Total:   72 [62]

[Other undated documents support the following as also having been shipped to the United States.]

| | | |
|---|---|---|
| J8M1 Shusui | 3 | [24] |
| G8N1 Renzan | 1 | |
| Ohka | 4 | |
| Kikka | 1 | |
| J8N1 [Supposedly Kikka] | 2 | |

Total:  83 [73] Navy aircraft.

[Note:  Information within brackets [ ]  is author added information.]

[*** :  Another original document, undated, gives these quantity figures, in brackets, which differ from the document reproduced here.]

What adjustments were made to these listings between the time they were developed in October and the boat departures in November and December of 1945, must remain an open issue. These lists show a total of 145 aircraft that were being readied to be ferried or moved for the subsequent voyage to the United States, yet according to Brundage, he recalls the final figure to be 108 aircraft. *Stars and Stripes* recorded that in November "an aggregate of 133 Japanese aircraft of all varieties" were *collected* for the purpose of investigation and study. A Japanese reference to a figure of 86 came from Mr. M H Miki, a person having had some responsibility over this shipment. All of these figures seem reasonable, and it is apparent that a full accounting will always remain an estimate.

Three aircraft carriers were involved with this post-war move of Japanese aircraft to America. The first boat-load to leave was on the USS *Barnes* (CVE-20), which departed Yokosuka on 16 November 1945, followed that same month by the USS *Core* (CVE-13). The last of these carriers for this collected assortment was the USS *Bogue* (CVE-9), which left the day after Christmas, arriving at Alameda Naval Base on 8 January 1946. Most, if not all, of the *Bogue's* deck cargo of Japanese aircraft continued with the ship through the Panama Canal to its destination at Newark, New Jersey on the east coast. Among the aircraft unloaded there was Japan's only surviving four-engined land-based bomber, the Nakajima G8N1 "Rita".

It is known that one or more of the small-size aircraft carriers encountered severe storms while making the eastward crossing of the Pacific. An unconfirmed report tells of some aircraft breaking loose from their moorings on one carrier deck as rough seas rolled the ship. In an attempt to prevent damage to the ship and other equipment, orders were given to cut many aircraft loose, allowing them to be tossed into the sea. That order, however, was countermanded before all were lost. This may account for the mystery of the disappearance of several types said to have been sent to the United States. The Mr. Miki, just mentioned, when referring to this storm at sea made the comment; "there was a whisper that reached my ear then, that the Kamikaze (devine wind) blew to prevent the aircraft from reaching the US!"

One interesting document pertaining to the recovery of Kawanishi H8K2 "Emily" flying-boats is worthy of recording here. Dated 27 September 1945, it was from the Commander-in-Chief, Air Force Advanced Echelon, Tokyo, to the War Department. No response was attached, but the answer would be obvious and could have been humorous:

> "Have 6 flyable transport versions of "Emily" available. If required, suggest either sending crews from United States or grant authority for use of Japanese crews to fly these aircraft across the Pacific." (!)

Because of poor Japanese aircraft maintenance by the end of the war, none of these aircraft would have been capable of such a challenging Pacific crossing by air. Eventually, however, one of these very large four-engine Kawanishi H8K2 flying-boats in the patrol bomber version was acquired for shipment to the United States. This "Emily" was located at Takuma Naval Base, headquarters for the 801st Kokutai, situated west of Takamatsu on Shikoku Island, Japan. In November 1945, it was flown by a Japanese crew with an American Navy pilot on board for the ride accompanied by a PBY Catalina escort. It landed in the harbour adjacent to Yokosuka and was loaded aboard the US Navy seaplane tender *Cumberland Sound* for the Pacific crossing. Upon reaching the west coast of the United States, it was off-loaded at Whidbey Island in Puget Sound, Washington State, in early December 1945. After close inspection, it was determined that it was in no condition for any ferry flight to its eventual east coast destination. Consequently, it was once again loaded aboard a ship and transported to NAS Norfolk, Virginia. The risk of losing the aircraft was too great to warrant such a ferry flight before experts could evaluate this aircraft, considered the best of the four-engine flying-boats of World War II. (In 1979 this aircraft was returned to Japan for lack of any apparent American interest.)

Only one inventory has been located of the aircraft carriers that transported the bulk of these aircraft to the United States. That inventory was that of the USS *Barnes,* that reported 45 Japanese aircraft as follows:

### INVENTORY OF JAPANESE AIRCRAFT ABOARD USS BARNES (CVE)

reported 3 November 1945

| Aircraft Type | Quantity | Serial Nos. |
| --- | --- | --- |
| Ki-44 Tojo | 2 | 1677, 1841 |
| Ki-45kai Nick | 1 | 4268 (at NASM) |
| Ki-46 Mod. III | 4 | 5444, 5453, 8053, 8058 |
| Ki-48 Lily | 1 | 1089 |
| Ki-84 Frank | 2 | 2366, 3060 |
| Ki-102b | 1 | 1116 |
| A6M7 Zeke 63 | 1 | 23186 (NASM loan to San Diego.) |
| B6N1 Jill 12 | 2 | 91112, 91210 |
| B6N2 Jill 13 | 1 | 5752 |

| | | |
|---|---|---|
| B7A Grace 11 | 2 | 278, 387 |
| C6N1 Myrt 11 | 4 | 735, 1308, 3379, 4161 (at NASM) |
| D4Y3 Judy 11 | 1 | 328 |
| D4Y3 Judy 12 | 1 | 3199 |
| D4Y4 Judy 33 | 2 | 1620, <u>1959</u><br>743 |
| D4Y4 Judy 43 | 4 | <u>1831</u>  <u>1833</u>  <u>3177</u>  <u>31537</u><br>307     309     917      713 |
| J1N1-S Irving | 1 | 7334 (at NASM) |
| J5N1 Tenrai | 2 | 11, 16 (parts at NASM) |
| J8H1 Shusui | 3 | 81, 403, 504 (at Planes of Fame) |
| M6A1-K Nanzan | 1 | <u>46</u><br>91 |
| N1K1-J George | 2 | 7287, 7317 |
| N1K2-J George | 4 | 71, 533, 5218, 5341 |
| P1Y Francis | 1 | 4867 |
| Q1W1 Lorna | <u>2</u> | 37, 170 |
| | 45 | |

Aboard the USS *Barnes* (CVE-20) are these Japanese aircraft lashed securely to the deck of this aircraft carrier bound for the United States in November 1945. Seen in this view are one each of "Irving", "Nick", "George", "Lily", "Dinah" and two "Myrts".
*(80-G-385840)*

Of the two "Betty" bombers which carried Japan's surrender envoys to meet with MacArthur's staff, this is the one that completed that mission by returning to its starting point. It stands forlornly at Kisarazu Air Base on the east bank of Tokyo Bay. MacArthur's instructions called for the two aircraft to be painted white and carry green crosses in place of the normal Japanese insignia. This historic aircraft was destroyed soon after this picture was taken 25 September 1945. *(SC 213261)*

Shorter range courier duties were performed with smaller aircraft such as this Kyushu K11W1 seen here at Sasabo Air Base on Kyushu in September 1945. This former operations trainer was an advanced trainer much like the North American AT-6/SNJ Texan although in size and appearance it was reminiscent of the North American O-47 observation aircraft. It has a fixed undercarriage.

*(USMC 138377)*

# CHAPTER VI
# BULLDOZING AND BURNING

## An Ignominious End

What to do with the numbers of Japanese aircraft that remained in Japan became a logistic problem. All military operations were permanently suspended and its military forces were being systematically inactivated. As far as flight operations for the Japanese was concerned, one element did remain. This became known for its short duration as the Green Cross Flight.

Soon after the cessation of hostilities, the need was recognized by the occupying forces that an air courier service was needed for the purpose of disseminating surrender directives to isolated forces. This could best be accomplished by Japanese pilots using their own equipment. To manage this, the Japanese Civil Aeronautics Bureau was given authority from the Occupation Forces Headquarters to resume a limited schedule of flight operations. From 15 September, thirteen days following the signing of the surrender terms, the Greater Japan Air Lines, Army and Navy, jointly started operations of the so-called Green Cross Flight with a total of twenty-seven aircraft. These included the Showa-built DC-3s, the Mitsubishi MC-20 and an assortment of smaller aircraft. Most of these aircraft were painted completely white, which also provided the prescribed white background upon which the identifying green cross insignia was directed to be painted in lieu of the red Rising Sun insignia. These markings were the same as those decreed by MacArthur's instructions when arranging for Japanese surrender envoys to fly to his headquarters in Manila for planning the terms of the surrender.

These civil flight operations came under the control of the Occupation Forces Headquarters. Initially, their function performed a valued service, but because of the large amount of air traffic over Japan in support of occupying forces, air traffic control communications became a problem with mixed languages. After several incidences which jeopardised air safety, the Green Cross Flight was ordered to discontinue its operations on 10 October 1945, and its aircraft were set aside.

As the occupation progressed, Japan's instruments of war were directed to be destroyed. With all flying activities abolished for the Japanese, there was no peace-time mission that these aircraft could perform. It was undoubtedly heartbreaking for any Japanese onlookers to have watched the bulldozers gather the remains of the once all-powerful air force into piles, as one would do wood-chips from the chopping block. This twisted mass was then put to the torch, and the fires belched forth a greasy, black cloud of smoke, to be seen for miles – an awesome sight repeated all over Japan.

The value of having Japanese crews with Japanese aircraft perform courier duties to carry communications to outlying Japanese forces after the surrender was recognized. Those aircraft performing this service would be painted white with green crosses. Here a Mitsubishi Ki-57II "Topsy" arriving in Mandalay, Burma, carrying surrender delegates.

Greasy black smoke and fire engulf the doomed Japanese "Gooney Bird", Allied Code name "Tabby", along with a line of Kawanishi N1K2 "George" fighters in the background. Once the Allies were certain that they had gathered the aircraft desired to be saved and evaluated, an order called for the destruction of all other Japanese aircraft that remained in Japan.

*(SC 221685)*

Neither the Japanese nor the Americans resisted this post-war destruction, even though the Japanese had little to say in the matter. They were eager to abolish anything that had to do with war. As a war trophy, the Americans retained a Kawasaki Ki-61 "Tony" and a Nakajima Ki-115 Tsurugi that were among the many at Yokota AB and displayed there for some years to come. Some time after the Occupation, these were turned back to Japanese ownership. The only other save was an Ohka 11 "Baka Bomb" that was carried to Johnson Air Base (now Iruma AB) from Atsugi Air Base, and used as a sign marker for the base. All other military aircraft surviving the war that remained in Japan were destroyed throughout the year and a half that followed.

## DISPOSAL OF JAPANESE AIRCRAFT

### As of 31 December, 1946

| Disposition | Fighter | Trainer | Transport | Misc. | Glider | Totals |
|---|---|---|---|---|---|---|
| Total to be disposed of | 720 | 1,118 | 69 | 10,797 | 31 | 12,735 |
| Destroyed | 511 | 788 | 22 | 8,429 | 16 | 9,766 |
| Scrapped | 35 | 39 | 1 | 1,016 | 2 | 1,092 |
| Allied Operations | 9 | | | 179 | | 188 |
| Intelligence | 27 | | | 73 | | 100 |
| Total Disposed | 582 | 827 | 23 | 9,697 | 17 | 11,146 |
| Total on hand | 138 | 291 | 46 | 1,100 | 14 | 1,589 |

(8,962 aircraft were located on Honshu, 2,637 on Kyushu, 631 on Shikoku, and the remainder [505] on Hokkaido.) (Source: Reports of General MacArthur, Volume I Supplement, p.136.)

The Green Cross Flight consisting of Japanese crews flying Japanese aircraft for courier duties, was terminated on 10 October 1945. With this, no further need was seen for aircraft such as this Showa-built DC-3. US Army personnel pour oil on the aircraft in preparation of setting it on fire. *(SC 221683)*

The bulldozer operator (right) pushes this "Nate" fighter into the nose of a Tachikawa "Hickory" trainer as if driving bumper-cars at a carnival. The mass destruction of Japanese aircraft may have taken on an almost playful air for some in the process. Admittedly, there was no graceful or caring way of accomplishing the destruction process.

The same "Hickory" in the foreground with the "Nate" that impacted its nose when pushed by a bulldozer, stands with Mitsubishi Ki-46 "Dinahs" of several models at an unknown air base. They will soon be pushed into a pile and burned.

American Army personnel are in the process of turning this Tachikawa Ki-9 "Spruce" basic trainer over on its back to ease wheel removal. Note the fabric sections that have been removed by souvenir hunters. To the left is a Kokusai Ki-86 Army trainer. This is a licence manufactured German Bucker Bu 131 Jungmann. *(SC 221340)*

Bulldozers continue the task of mounding Japanese aircraft for the final fire of destruction. This operation is taking place at Niigata AB on the north coast of central Honshu. Many in view here are advanced Army trainers, most of which were planned for the final phase of the war as kamikaze aircraft.

*(SC 225913)*

Wheels and tyres were removed from many aircraft like these Ki-9s to be given to the Japanese for use on farm implements. An item such as this in post-war Japan became a valued assistance in replacing even the simplest of farm tools. *(SC 221585)*

It appeared that wheels were the only item considered to be of value for retention in the destruction process of Japanese aircraft. In the right foreground is one of the few examples of a Kokusai Ki-76 "Stella" to be photographed. These were an adaptation of the Fieseler Fi 156 Storch of which production figures are not known. *(SC 225911)*

Wheel-less trainers can only be pushed on their backs by the bulldozer crews. The insignia on the fin of the Tachikawa Ki-55 "Ida" in the foreground is that of "Ni" signifying Niigata, the training school and air base to which these trainers were assigned. Reportedly, the J was painted on by Americans. *(SC 221341)*

The twisted remains of these aircraft are hardly recognizable. The twin-engine centre wing section in the foreground is that of a Showa-built DC-3. It is estimated that over 17,000 Japanese aircraft were destroyed in this fashion after the war on the main islands of Japan. *(SC 221338)*

The igniting fuel is poured over the wing of an aircraft in preparation of its burning by a Japanese worker at Kyoto. In the background is a Tachikawa Ki-54 "Hickory" advanced trainer of which the cockpit windscreen has been demolished as are all windows.

*(SC 223656)*

The final remains of a N1K1-J "George" fighter go up in flames and heavy smoke. As fires like this burn, explosions from gas tanks rip open the structures. This photo was taken on 31 October 1945, most likely on Kyushu.

*(SC 221690)*

Dope and fabric wings fuel the fire as this mass of Japanese aircraft are part of the many destroyed. In the foreground are Tachikawa Ki-9 "Spruce" basic trainers of the Japanese Army. Large numbers of this type of aircraft were equipped to expend themselves in kamikaze attacks when the Allied invasion was to begin.

*(SC 223706)*

Army troops of the 5th Ordnance Battalion, 24th Infantry Division watch with Japanese workers as more stacked aircraft are put to the torch. This process of destroying the bulk of Japanese aircraft that remained after the surrender extended well into 1946 because of the magnitude of the project.

*(SC 221561)*

The American forces that first occupied Yokota Air Base set this Nakajima Ki-115 Tsurugi kamikaze aircraft to one side as their own war trophy. It remained here in front of their barracks for several years. Eventually it was returned to the Japanese and it now resides in semi-storage at a Tokyo high school.

A plume of black smoke rises from these Kawanishi N1K1-J and N1K2-J "George" fighters at an unidentified Japanese Air Field on 31 October 1945. The quantity of fighters clustered here could approximate one Hikotai (squadron) strength of aircraft. At the left is another Green Cross Flight "Tabby" (DC-3 equivalent) aircraft, now slightly damaged and awaiting its turn to be torched.

*(SC 221691)*

The unloaded "Patsy" is towed to a parking area to await further disposition. Unloading of Japanese aircraft such as this took place at several shipyards along the Atlantic as well as the Pacific coast.

After the Pacific Ocean crossing and a cruise through the Panama Canal on board an aircraft carrier, this Tachikawa Ki-74 "Patsy" is being off-loaded at Newark, New Jersey. The dark coating for protection against the sea air is quite disguising.

# CHAPTER VII

# MAKING THE CUT

## Wanted, Yet Not Wanted

Considerable effort has been placed upon learning what had become of these Japanese aircraft after their arrival in the United States. Recognizing that these were acquired for research purposes, there are few documents in US government files that support only little attention having been given to these aircraft in that regard. Records for showing locations to where these aircraft were placed have disappeared from archival files, if ever there in the first place. US Navy logs of the transporting ships have been checked in hopes of finding the manifests telling of the aircraft being carried on each ship and the ports at which they were discharged. No records of this type have surfaced.

What is known is that these ships stopped at numerous ports on the west coast from Whidbey Island NAS in Washington State, to Alameda and San Diego in California, with possibly others in-between. The loads they discharged ended up at some inland stations such as El Toro and New Orleans. What resulted at these destinations can only be left to conjecture. Supposedly, they were being dispersed to the various services and their laboratories where evaluations could be made on selected aircraft.

"Rita" arrived at Wright-Patterson AFB for evaluation while still clad in its orange paint that was typical of Japanese Navy aircraft that were still undergoing tests. Evaluation in the United States consisted of two or three flights before the project was cancelled. It was felt that nothing was to be gained compared to the risk in further evaluation. After about two years at Wright Patterson, "Rita" was scrapped along with several other foreign aircraft. *(H Levy via P Bowers)*

The same held true for those unloaded on the East Coast after their passage through the Panama Canal. Ports such as Philadelphia and Newark, New Jersey and Norfolk are confirmed unloading points. Newark seemed the most used port for discharging aircraft destined for US Army Air Forces evaluation, since this was the closest port to the very inland Air Matériel Center at Wright Field, Dayton, Ohio.

To assist with the distribution of these aircraft, perhaps after the fact in some cases, was a catalogue prepared by the Air Matériel Command that is seemingly the earliest official document that listed Foreign Equipment. Publication date of the Catalogue was 10 March 1946, and it was here that most of the aircraft identification numbers of specific aircraft types were recorded.

The catalogue consisted of one-page basic descriptions and photographs of each type made available to the aerospace industry. The cover page of this document tells the nature of the availability of these aircraft, and is quoted here in part:

> "In order to further the advancement of the aeronautical industry and to further the national defense, the equipment described in these pages is available to interested activities for the express purpose of experimental research, test, development, display, or gift. However, before shipment can be made, it is necessary that (1) the government know and approve the purpose for which the equipment is desired, and (2) a bailment contract be executed protecting the proprietary interest of the government. If the test to be conducted will necessitate eventual destruction of the property, no return of the equipment is required nor does the government expect reimbursement for the property destroyed. If the test does not require destruction, the material will be returned. Reports on findings will be submitted to the government. Transportation costs will be borne by the government to and from the point of destination indicated on the bailment contract."

This Aichi E16A1 "Paul" ended up at Floyd Bennett Field, a Naval Air Station near New York City. Note the split-type dive brakes on the float main strut. Tail marking indicates that this aircraft once belonged to the 634th Kokutai. There is no record of this type having been flown in the United States. *(NASM A47648)*

Anacostia Naval Air Station, Washington, D.C. was a major rebuilding facility for the Air Technical Intelligence Center for Japanese aircraft. This work was in conjunction with that accomplished at Wright Field in enemy aircraft evaluation. Here under rebuild a "Tony", "Zeke 21", and a "Dinah" for flight evaluation. Work of this magnitude terminated soon after hostilities ended.

*(B Clark via NASM 77-2706)*

The Kawanishi H8K2 "Emily" that was shipped separately to the United States was probably the most useful of the post-war acquired Japanese aircraft. Recognized as the most efficient four-engine flying boat of World War Two, its hull configuration was thoroughly evaluated in many taxi tests. Valuable findings were later applied to US Navy's P5M Marlin, P6M Seamaster and R3Y Tradewind flying-boats. *(80-G-448781)*

For Air Force accounting purposes, most foreign equipment was assigned an identifying number, preceded by "FE" ("Foreign Equipment"). With the forming of the Foreign Technology Division, T-2, a few months following the war, the prefix to these numbers was changed to "T2". There is no known complete listing of all the FE/T2 numbers, thus it is only speculation as to which types and quantities of aircraft may have been on that list. Consecutive numbering would not be a help in this determination since parts and equipment obtained from foreign sources were also within this same numbering system. In addition, not all of the numbered aircraft and equipment may necessarily have arrived in the US.

It is interesting to note that the few Japanese aircraft which were assigned numbers prefixed by "FE", possibly indicates their existence of some to be in the United States prior to the end of the war; however, photos of the Japanese aircraft in the US do not show the T2 prefix on any of these aircraft. Those aircraft tested by the Navy seemingly deleted the "T2" and used the prefix "N" to the assigned T2 number.

While the war was in progress, the Navy conducted the greater share of testing and evaluation of the captured Japanese aircraft. Within a matter of months following termination of the war, nearly all activities with foreign equipment became the responsibility of the Army Air Forces. There is no evidence that Navy-owned Japanese equipment was later transferred to the Air Force.

When tests were completed, the "Emily" was moved to Norfolk NAS, Virginia and stored for the National Air Museum. It was connected to a life support system that kept dry air pumped through its structure while its outside was wrapped in a protective coating. It was never claimed by the museum and later returned to Japan.

Also located at Norfolk NAS was this Aichi B7A1 Carrier Attack Bomber, "Grace", photographed 15 May 1947. Four of this type were reported having been shipped to the United States. Components of this one disappeared, one by one, and the aircraft was eventually scrapped. The one that does survive and is part of the collection of the National Air and Space Museum was obtained from the Navy at Alameda NAS, California in 1963.

After the war, interest diminished in the evaluation of enemy war equipment. Cutbacks in military spending and manpower brought about the necessary scrapping of much equipment, foreign and American alike. Herein lies the probable answer as to what happened to the majority of Japanese aircraft brought to America. Most had left Japan in what was supposed to be those in best condition, yet that was undoubtedly marginal. Many would best be described as in need of considerable re-work after their sea voyage and lack of attention after their arrival, as they were undoubtedly left in the open. They arrived only to have their internal accessories and equipment removed by swarms of inspection parties whose purpose was to "evaluate" certain components. Once this was accomplished, the scrap heaps were usually the next stopping point for these objects. Some were used in conjunction with Bond drives that boosted "Victory Bonds" in place of the popular name of "War Bonds".

A Fighter Conference was held at the Navy Air Test Center, Patuxent River, attended by some of the top test pilots in the armed forces. For evaluation and comparison tests, a number of former enemy aircraft, mostly the fighter types, were flown by many of the participants. At the conclusion of the conference an order was given to make these aircraft unflyable, following which many were scrapped or sent to the Naval Proving Ground, Dahlgren, Virginia. Normally, aircraft sent to Dahlgren became targets for weapons, both ground and air. A Navy Chief Petty Officer carried out his orders to "make them unflyable" by sawing off their engines!

While this fate was similar to many examples of captured or confiscated enemy aircraft, the Army Air Forces had initiated a programme that had to do with saving a number of selected aircraft types that had participated in World War II. Because of the far-sightedness of General H H "Hap" Arnold, commanding general of the USAAF, he recognized the educational and historic value in having for study and exhibit, actual aircraft of that war to show significant aeronautical advancements that the war had brought about. He directed that one of every major aircraft type under the control of the Army Air Forces be set aside for the future. These included many foreign types, both Allied and Axis, that were brought to America for evaluation. He encouraged the Navy to do likewise, which they did.

The gathering point for these aircraft became a huge, government-owned aircraft assembly building at Park Ridge, Illinois that once was used to produce Douglas C-54 Skymasters during the war. The adjacent runways were those of Orchard Place Airport, eventually renamed O'Hare Field in honour of Marine ace E H "Butch" O'Hare, and is now Chicago International Airport. Along with USAAF aircraft that were selected came test aircraft from Freeman Field, Indiana, where most of the Japanese and German types were evaluated by the Army. This overall grouping constituted a very impressive collection of aircraft that documented the types used during this extensive war-time period.

The collection needed a purpose and a future because of its great importance. With the advice and active assistance of General Arnold, the Honorable Jennings Randolph, then Representative, later Senator, for West Virginia, authored a measure that would establish the National Air Museum. With the approval of Congress, this was signed into law by President Harry S Truman on 12 August 1946. One of the purposes for this museum was to relieve the military from museum responsibilities. Because of this, the collection of military aircraft at Park Ridge was transferred from the USAAF to the National Air Museum (NAM). Soon to follow was the offer of selected examples from the US Navy which included Japanese aircraft as well.

At the onset, the collection of military aircraft being offered consisted of 220 of all types. Of this, the Army listed fifty-four Japanese aircraft available to the museum, while the Navy had set aside twenty-seven Japanese aircraft to be saved for the museum at various stations where they had been dispersed for various reasons.

It can be understandable that after a prolonged war, interest in war-making machines quickly fades. There were few aviation museums as we know them today that stood ready to receive these Japanese, or other aircraft considered historic today. These aircraft gathered at Norfolk NAS had no takers and were set off to one side of the base. The "Rex" and "George" were preserved (background) while the "Frank" and "Jill", two of Japan's best warplanes, were scrapped.

Another rare find at Norfolk was this Kugisho (Yokosuka) D4Y3 Suisei known as "Judy". These were deadly dive bombers in the hands of capable Japanese crews. This one stands neglected at Norfolk in the late 1940s, lacking American understanding of its technical significance for being retained. None of the eight "Judys" in two models sent to the United States remain.

For those that remember this Kawanishi N1K2-J "George" located near the perimeter fence at Anacostia NAS, Washington, DC, in the late 1940s, its existence is now legendary. It sat adjacent to a Messerschmitt Me 262. Vandals and souveniring soon took its toll of both, and they were eventually scrapped.

*(NASM 90-16490)*

Other cast-offs at Norfolk is a second Kawanishi N1K1 "Rex" seaplane fighter and the two-place "Baka Bomb", Both of these aircraft are in storage at the National Air and Space Museum but in much worse condition than seen here.

This Nakajima C6N1 "Myrt" is poised on the flight line of what is presumed to be Olmsted Air Base at Harrisburg, Pennsylvania. It was there that many Japanese aircraft were mechanically prepared for flight evaluation. "Myrt" appears ready for air ferry to a flight evaluation base such as Freemen Field, Seymour, Indiana, Wright-Patterson AFB, Ohio, Patuxent River NAS, Maryland, and others. *(NASM 47763-B)*

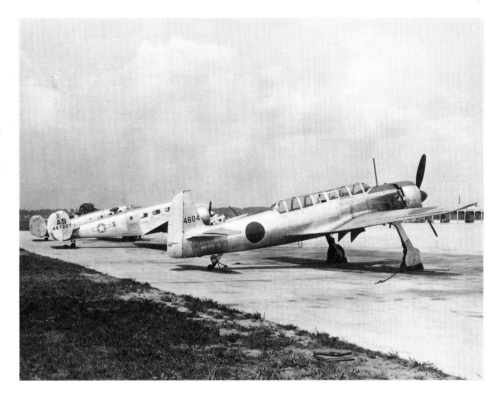

Of the four "Myrts" sent to the United States, this one was selected for retention in the National Aeronautical Collection. At this point in 1951, it rests outdoors at the museum's storage location at Park Ridge, Illinois, awaiting disassembly and movement to the museum's next storage location at Silver Hill, Maryland. *(D Menard)*

Many of the aircraft at Park Ridge were able to be stored indoors from the time they were accepted from the US Army Forces in 1948 until evicted a few years later. A number of aircraft were deleted from the collection at this point for lack of funds and storage room in which to handle the entire collection. Aircraft such as "Tojo", two "Franks", "Betty" and others were lost in this process.

*(NASM A-5882)*

In various parts of the United States, former enemy aircraft began to appear in public locations, no longer needed by the military. This Mitsubishi J2M3 "Jack", a Navy fighter, appeared in a Los Angeles park in the late 1940s. It was soon given to the Planes of Fame Museum and received the care that it deserved.

## JAPANESE AIRCRAFT ONCE SAVED IN THE US

When the US military services concluded their needs for the Japanese aircraft evaluations, they were set aside for museum purposes as were many other US as well as foreign aircraft on hand at the end of the war. Eventually, a majority of these aircraft were to make up the collection of the newly-formed National Air Museum, now the National Air and Space Museum (NASM) in Washington, D.C. The following Japanese aircraft types have been extracted from that overall list of aircraft originally on hand and available by the USAF as of 1 May 1949. Most were eventually deleted during the transfer process for many and extensive reasons, mostly economical.

(Note: Bold print entries indicate those aircraft that remain in the NASM collection.)

| Aircraft Type | Air Technical Intelligence Number |
|---|---|
| Kawanishi N1K2-J George | |
| Kawanishi N1K1 Rex | T2-N324 |
| Kawasaki Ki-45 Kai Nick | (S-14) T2-3303 |
| **Kawasaki Ki-45 Kai Nick** | **T2-701** |
| Kawasaki Ki-48 Lily | T2-1205 |
| Kawasaki Ki-61 Tony | |
| Kawasaki Ki-100 Tony | T2-314 |
| Kawasaki Ki-100 Tony | T2-315 |
| Kawasaki Ki-102 Randy | FE-304 |
| Kawasaki Ki-102 Randy | FE-308 |
| Kugisho D4Y4 Judy | T2-N1203 |
| Kugisho D4Y4 Judy | T2-1201 |
| **Kugisho P1Y1 Francis** | **T2-1702** |
| Kugisho Ohka, Baka | FE-43006 |
| Kyushu Q1W1 Lorna | T2-4810 |
| **Kyushu J7W1 Shinden** | **T2-326** |
| Mitsubishi Ki-46 Dinah | T2-4801 |
| Mitsubishi Ki-46 Dinah | T2-4802 |
| Mitsubishi Ki-49 Helen | T2-1705 |
| Mitsubishi Ki-67 Peggy | T2-2201 |
| Mitsubishi Ki-83 | T2-151 |
| **Mitsubishi A6M5 Zeke** | **T2-130** |
| Mitsubishi A6M7 Zeke | T2-N311 |
| Mitsubishi A6M7 Zeke | T2-N322 |
| Mitsubishi J2M5 Jack | T2-N320 |
| Mitsubishi J2M5 Jack | T2-N321 |
| **Mitsubishi G4M3 Betty** (nose only) | **T2-2205** |
| Nakajima Ki-43 Oscar | T2-6430* |
| Nakajima Ki-43 Oscar | |
| Nakajima Ki-44 Tojo | T2-N303 |
| Nakajima Ki-84 Frank | T2-302 |
| Nakajima Ki-84 Frank | T2-1446 |
| Nakajima Ki-87 (High Alt. Ftr.) | T2-153 |
| **Nakajima Ki-115 Tsurugi** | **T2-156** |

| | |
|---|---|
| **Nakajima C6N2 Myrt** | **T2-N4803** |
| Nakajima C6N2 Myrt | T2-4804 |
| **Nakajima J1N1 Irving** | **T2-N700** |
| Rikugun Ki-93 (Ground Supp. Ftr.) | T2-152 |
| Tachikawa Ki-74 Patsy | T2-2208 |
| Tachikawa Ki-77 (Long range) | T2-154 |
| Tachikawa Ki-94 (Hi. Alt. Ftr.) | T2-150 |

Japanese aircraft listed (apart from others) as stored elsewhere by the Air Force in 1949 and available to National Air Museum.

| | |
|---|---|
| Kawasaki Ki-48 Lily | T2-1202 |
| Kawasaki Ki-102 Randy | FE-309 |
| Kawasaki Ki-102 Randy | FE-310 |
| Kyushu Q1W1 Lorna | T2-N4800 |
| Kyushu Q1W1 Lorna | T2-4811 |
| Mitsubishi Ki-46 Dinah | T2-4806 |
| Mitsubishi Ki-46 Dinah | T2-4807 |
| Mitsubishi Ki-46 Dinah | T2-4812 |
| Mitsubishi Ki-67 Peggy | T2-2202 |
| Mitsubishi Ki-67 Peggy | T2-2203 |
| Mitsubishi Ki-67 Peggy | T2-2204 |
| Nakajima C6N2 Myrt | T2-4808 |
| Tachikawa Ki-74 Patsy | T2-2209 |

Correspondence from the US Navy also listed Japanese aircraft being saved for museum purposes and available on call for the National Air Museum. Included were an identifying number and station location where stored.

| | | |
|---|---|---|
| Aichi E13A1 Jake | | Seattle |
| Aichi E16A1 Paul | 70 | Brooklyn |
| **Aichi M6A1 Seiran** | 47 | From Alameda |
| **Aichi B7A2 Grace** | 52 | Norfolk |
| Aichi M6A1-K Nanzan | A-3 | Seattle |
| Kawanishi N1K1 Rex | 40 | Philadelphia |
| Kawanishi N1K1 Rex | 45 | Boston |
| Kawanishi N1K1-J George | 41 | Dahlgren, Va |
| Kawanishi N1K2-J George | 19 | Dahlgren, Va |
| Kawanishi N1K2-J George | 20 | Dahlgren, Va |
| Kawanishi N1K2-J George | 32 | Willow Grove * |
| Kawanishi H8K2 Emily | | Norfolk |
| Kugisho D4Y3 Judy | | Charleston |
| Kugisho D4Y3 Judy | 22 | Dahlgren, Va |
| Kugisho D4Y4 Judy | 26 | Dahlgren, Va |
| Kugisho D4Y4 Judy | 42 | Charleston |
| Mitsubishi A6M5 Zeke | 21 | New Orleans |
| Mitsubishi A6M7 Zeke | 14 | Willow Grove * |

| | | |
|---|---|---|
| Mitsubishi J8M1 Shusui | 24 | Glenview |
| Nakajima B5N2 Kate | | Seattle |
| Nakajima B6N2 Jill | 12 | Willow Grove * |
| Nakajima Ki-84 Frank | 119 | Glenview |
| Nakajima Ki-84 Frank | 108 | Jacksonville |
| **Nakajima Kikka** | | Patuxent R. |
| Nakajima Kikka | | Unk. |
| Nakajima Kikka | A-103 | San Diego |
| Nakajima Kikka | A-104 | Willow Grove |

(Note: Asterisk indicates acquired later by the National Air and Space Museum and currently possessed.)

The staff of the fledgling museum at this time consisted of approximately five members, secretaries included. There was no separate funding with which to work, let alone having a place in which to place this enormous collection. As it was, the five or six acquisitions of civilian type aircraft acquired during this transitional period were also sent to Park Ridge for storage since the museum had no other storage location.

The future remained grim for the new museum as far as rapid expansion to care for this collection was concerned. This left only one alternative, and that was to be selective at reducing the size of this assortment, even if it meant to forsake the objective for which these aircraft were gathered in the first place, i.e. to save one of each type of significant aircraft from that wartime period.

To make this selection, a small committee was formed that would evaluate which aircraft would be suitable for museum needs. Minutes from those meetings were extensive and reflected the reasons for deletions and retentions. What is obvious from these records, however, is that no one on the committee was familiar with Japanese aircraft based upon some of the reasoning that was recorded. As one example, "since a Ki-100 had been selected, the Type 100 is considered to be redundant." As any scholar of Japanese aircraft is aware, there were great differences, the Ki-100 is a Kawasaki Ki-61 "Tony" with a radial engine, while the Type 100 reconnaissance was a twin-engine Ki-46 "Dinah". Typographical errors also crept into the selection system, eliminating any form of reference material or evaluation. One very rare Kikka was carried as *Eilka* and deemed an "insignificant" type and a second one also eliminated was referred to as *Japanese twin-jet fighter* as having no positive identity.

The bigger Japanese aircraft also missed making the cut for being saved, such examples being one or more "Sallys", "Peggys", "Helens", Ki-83 twin-engine long-range high-altitude fighter, and others of technological significance and historic value. One of the most regrettable historical as well as technological ✶ losses was the Tachikawa Ki-77. This was a twin-engine pressurized-cabin aircraft of which the construction for two was started before the war. *Asahi Shimbun* (Newspaper) was the sponsor of this project of building an aircraft that could fly non-stop from Tokyo to New York City in 1940. This was to be a goodwill flight to commemorate the 2600th year of the Japanese Empire. Because of war clouds, the project was terminated, but the Army later resumed their construction in hopes of using them for establishing an air link with Germany. In the first attempt at such an international flight, the aircraft was lost

✶ PAGE 109 (PICTURE)

An aircraft that has always attracted public attention at Willow Grove NAS, Pennsylvania has been this Kawanishi N1K1 "Rex", shown here in 1993. This aircraft is looked upon as being the most successful seaplane fighter ever placed in operational service. It remains to this day in unprotected outdoor exhibit.

somewhere over the Indian Ocean after departing Singapore in July 1943. Speculation is that this was caused by an interception made by a British fighter since a British claim was made on that date and in that vicinity on an unknown type of Japanese aircraft. The second aircraft flew a closed course unofficial distance in Manchuria of 8,900 nautical miles, with enough fuel remaining for an additional 1,080 nm. This total exceeded the route mileage between Tokyo and New York by 2,800 nm, giving the aircraft a fuel reserve of 40 per cent. This aircraft survived the war, was transported to the United States with the other post-war shipments, and was never recognized for its significance until years after it had been scrapped.

There were many other tragic losses among the eighty-one candidates, of which only eleven, plus the severed nose section of a "Betty", were brought into the collection by the National Air Museum in 1947. Only a few of those not selected were spared the scrap salvage yard, and those few have survived to this day. One major save was by Edward Maloney of the "Planes of Fame" museum in California. He was able to purchase from the scrap dealer, the Nakajima Ki-84 "Frank" that had been test-flown and transported from the Philippines. That aircraft has since been sold to an owner in Japan. A "Baka Bomb" from the would-be collection went to the Victory Air Museum near Chicago by the same purchase method and is now at the Yankee Air Museum, Chino, California. A "George", "Jill", "Zeke 63" and a "Rex" unclaimed by the museum from the Navy went to Willow Grove NAS, Pennsylvania. Since then, all but the "Rex" have been saved by NASM when on the verge of destruction from weathering. The unclaimed "George" that was offered from the USAAF collection is most likely the example that now resides in the Air Force Museum. The once ignored Ki-43 "Oscar" by NAM was acquired by that museum soon after making the selection decisions.

For that early, transitional time, one must place themselves in the position of those having to make these decisions to appreciate this selection task that confronted them. Those charged with making these decisions were sincerely concerned about the responsibility placed upon them. By today's standards and knowledge of Japanese aircraft, the decisions might have been entirely different, but in the years during and immediately following the war, very little was known about Japanese aircraft. For example, the Shinden described in the committee minutes was considered a Japanese "copy" of the XP-55 Ascender. Neither design factions were aware of the others endeavours which makes for an excellent example of how technologies paralleled each other during a given time period.

Over the years since the early selections were made, the collection of Japanese aircraft within the National Air and Space Museum (NASM) has not only remained stable, but regained three of its losses by acquiring those from Willow Grove NAS. Restorations of these aircraft at the museum is extremely slow, having only restored the Zero Fighter and the "Irving" since 1947. Within the first few years that these Japanese aircraft were in the United States when many were designated to be scrapped, their engines were removed and saved by the museum. Instrument panels, radios, bomb sights and similar equipment were selectively removed from these aircraft and added to the museum collection where most reside to this day. This collection is looked upon by the world as the largest repository of Japanese World War II technology. It would be unpardonable if the National Air and Space Museum were to allow any further reduction or dispersal of this rare collection, but instead, should care for this source for study by conserving it and preparing it for display for all to see.

Several former enemy aircraft were placed on outdoor display at Willow Grove NAS, Pennsylvania when evaluations were completed at several locations. This sole surviving Nakajima B6N2 "Jill", shown here in September 1959, may well have been evaluated at the nearby Naval Aircraft Factory. Prior to its near fatal destruction from the elements, it was transferred to the National Air and Space Museum in August 1981.

Countries formerly occupied by the Japanese were obliged to rebuild their air forces with what was immediately available to them. In the case of China, a large variety of Japanese military aircraft were left behind when their former enemy returned to their homeland. This Kawasaki Ki-61-kai-C "Tony" was one aircraft placed in Chinese service but with even less success than the Japanese experienced because of chronic engine problems. Photo was taken at Nanyuan Airfield, Peiping, September 1945.
*(R Bueschel via R Seely)*

This Chinese-marked Ki-61 "Tony" retains olive green camouflage spray painted over natural metal presumably applied while in Japanese service. The former unit markings have been painted over. This "Tony" photographed at Peiping on 16 November 1945, was recaptured a few days after this photo was taken by Chinese Communists. *(P Bowers via R Seely)*

# CHAPTER VIII
# FOREIGN SERVICE

## Japanese Aircraft in Other Air Forces

The Nakajima Ki 43 "Oscar" was a fighter of significant quantity to serve in the Chinese People's Liberation Army Air Force. At least seventeen Japanese Army Air Force Sentais had operated Oscars as their basic equipment in China and Manchuria during the war period. Most were withdrawn before the war ended, but significant numbers of aircraft remained in China. *(R Seely)*

When the war ended, Japanese forces occupied a number of countries in the Far East and South-east Asia. In these countries were combat air units of both the Japanese Army and Navy. These units had diminished toward the end of the war, not only through attrition, but in a series of scheduled withdrawals of both equipment and pilots to the main islands of Japan in readiness for the expected Allied invasion. According to the US Strategic Bombing Survey, titled *Japanese Air Power,* they reported that 1,000 Japanese aircraft remained in South-east Asia in various conditions, and that sixty-five per cent were trainers. While these figures have merit, unspecified numbers of aircraft remained in China, Manchuria, Korea, and other areas outside Japan that were unreported. Many were combat aircraft, including fighters and bombers.

Many of these aircraft were unserviceable and remained that way for lack of parts, a situation that jeopardized Japan's air power throughout the war. The more serviceable aircraft left behind by the Japanese were quickly placed into service by newly-formed governments that seized upon the opportunity of utilizing this treasure trove of Japanese equipment for their own air forces. This generally made them the most powerful military forces in their area.

### Chinese Air Force

In newly liberated Manchukuo (at the time known as Manchuria in the west), a Chinese province occupied by the Russians at the conclusion of the war, the Soviets secretly turned much of the surviving Japanese equipment over to the Chinese Communists. This was an illegal and clandestine act which was strictly against the terms of the Japanese surrender. The materials were to have gone instead to the recognized and established Chinese Nationalist Government, a UN member. For the first time, the Chinese Communists possessed modern military equipment in volume, but they did not know how to use it. In this time of confusion, Japanese and former Manchukuoan pilots and technicians, not knowing what to do next, signed up as mercenaries with the Chinese Communists by the hundreds and both manned the aircraft and trained the Chinese in their use. The new Communist Chinese Air Force was theoretically the strongest air arm in northern China through the use of Japanese military aircraft.

Relatively modern in many ways, this equipment was far newer than had been available to the once poorly equipped Army prior to the end of the Pacific War. Now, their fighter aircraft consisted of Nakajima Ki-43 "Oscars" and Ki-84 "Franks" that had formerly been with the 48th, 104th, and 204th Japanese Army fighter Sentais stationed in Manchukuo. There were also an uncounted number of Nakajima Ki-44 "Tojo" and Kawasaki Ki-61 "Tony" fighters that had been stationed in northern China. Approximately 100 Mitsubishi Ki-51 "Sonia" single-engine fixed-undercarriage ground attack aircraft, along with Kawasaki Ki-48 "Lily" twin-engine light bombers that had been used by the Japanese in anti-guerrilla operations were included in these recoveries, filling out the Communists ranks.

Of more immediate importance to the Communists were the many transports and trainers obtained at Mukden and Harbin, the major Manchukuoan Japanese Army Air Force bases. Japanese pilots that entered into the Communist service known as the People's Liberation Army Air Force (PLAAF) provided the field armies with the first air-lift capability they had ever experienced by flying Nakajima Ki-34 "Thora" and Tachikawa Ki-54 "Hickory" twin-engine transports. A larger transport but in fewer numbers was the Mitsubishi Ki-57 "Topsy". This was a transport version of the very respected Ki-21 "Sally" that was so visible in Chinese skies during the war. This fast transport for its day could carry eleven passengers.

The propeller of this "Tojo" was probably removed in compliance with the surrender agreements, however, no time was lost by China in applying their own insignia on these aircraft. Seen here in addition to the "Tojo" at Peiping on 17 November 1945 are a Kawasaki Ki-61 "Tony", Nakajima Ki-84 "Frank", and to the right is a Nakajima-Fokker Super Universal transport. *(Dick Seeley)*

Among the most valuable aircraft thus acquired were those that would be needed to train their own Chinese pilots, including Tachikawa Ki-55 "Ida" and Manshu Ki-97b single-engine monoplanes. These single-engine trainers were complemented by Tachikawa Ki-54a twin-engine Hickory advanced trainers acquired at Mukden. By October 1945, the Chinese Communists had all the equipment they needed for modern flight-training schools in their newly-occupied province of Manchuria, a starting point from which they would launch their successful invasion of mainland China.

The Nationalist Chinese were not without Japanese equipment in their air force. Equipment much of the same as that turned over to the Communists was also captured by the Nationalists throughout what had been the Japanese area of occupation and placed into service. Nakajima Ki-44 "Tojo" fighters from the 9th Fighter Sentai at Nanking were taken into inventory by the Nationalist Chinese as were Ki-84 "Franks" found in Nanking, Hankow and Peking. Stripped of their wartime paint, they went into service a second time, now clad in the white-and-blue starburst insignia of the Chinese Air Force. A number of Ki-48 "Lily" bombers of the 16th and 90th Light Bomber Sentais also at Nanking, Peking, and Hankow, were taken over by the Nationalists, but seemingly they made little active use of these former Japanese bombers. The Nationalists were in a better position to use this equipment because of their previous flight training during the war years, but their numbers in Japanese equipment were far less than that of the Communist forces.

These 1938 vintage Mitsubishi Ki-30 "Anns" were once the backbone of Japanese Army light bombers in China. They remained in operational service in China and Manchuria until the end of the Pacific War. Repainted with Chinese markings at wars end, they became early equipment for the new air force of the Chinese Communists. These Ki-30s were photographed at Nan Yuan Airfield, Peking (Beijing), China in November 1945. *(USMC 226321)*

The situation in mainland China was of major turmoil with two Chinese governments trying to take control of the country. Flexing its muscles with its new air power, the Communists were the first to use this strength. In May, 1946, unmarked fighters of Japanese design came in low and strafed a Nationalist armoured train north of Mukden, in Manchuria. The attack killed at least 100 persons. No one doubted that the pilots were Japanese since it was well known that the Chinese Communists did not have pilots trained well enough to be capable of handling modern fighter aircraft. It was at this time that the Nationalists had begun to move in and reclaim the territory in northern China and Manchuria that was first occupied by the Communists. A cease fire that began 13 January 1947, had little effect, and by 15 April the Communists went on the offensive again after refusing to take part in a coalition government.

With American aid placed on the side of the Nationalist Chinese in accordance with the prescribed Allied terms that stemmed from the previous war, all wartime Japanese equipment in China was instantly made obsolete. For the older Japanese aircraft, inherent mechanical problems in the air, compounded with maintenance problems on the ground and an end to replacement parts was a pressing reason to phase-out this equipment at the earliest time possible. The Communists were forced to replace their equipment with the obvious answer – Russian aircraft. How long any of these former World War II Japanese aircraft remained in service can only be left to speculation, but no doubt there were traces of these aircraft in both services until the early 1950s.

Some Japanese that were in China at the time of the surrender remained there as instructors to the Chinese in the operation of their former aircraft. Here a mix of American Marines, Japanese, and Chinese discuss the Kawasaki Ki-48 "Lily" now in Chinese service at Nan Yuan Airfield, Peking (Beijing), China, December 1945.

*(USMC 226611)*

Japan's best fighter to go into foreign service was the Nakajima Ki-84 "Frank". Numbers were relatively few. This one served on the side of the Chinese Communists before changing to star-and-bar insignia. *(P Bowers via R Seely)*

The Chinese Armies, both Nationalist and Communists, were left with a number of Japanese transports which gave them the mobility neither had ever experienced before. The Mitsubishi Ki-57 "Topsy" was the largest quantity transport to fall into Chinese hands. In civil passenger service, these were known as MC-20, able to carry eleven passengers. *(R Bueschel via R Seely)*

This Nakajima-Fokker Super Universal Transport may well have been built in Manchuria by Manshu Koku KK for the civil air routes in that country. These were six passenger transports for Manchurian Airways Co Limited whose operation also ended when Japan surrendered. The Chinese pressed this well-used Super Universal into their military service. *(R Seely)*

The strength of the Red Chinese Army's bomber force was made up of Kawasaki Ki-48 "Lily" light bombers from former Japanese bomber Sentais. These bombers stationed in China at the time of Japan's surrender were relatively small in number. This line of "Lilys" was photographed in Nanking, August 1946. *(Campbell Archives)*

The later version of the Showa-built DC-3 was this L2D3 transport. In addition to a rearranged crew compartment which accounts for added windows, it was powered by Kinsei 1,300 hp engines giving it greatly improved performance over all other DC-3 types. This Chinese-conscripted L2D3 stands alongside the previously pictured "Topsy" at West Field, Peking (Beijing), China sometime between April and November 1946.

*(D Lucabaugh via R Seely)*

This service-worn Ki-57 "Topsy" now in Chinese service, appears to be ready to load passengers. Although Japanese aircraft were relatively plentiful in China at the end of the war, the lack of a supply system for aircraft maintenance parts, made their service life limited to the end of the 1940s.

*(R Bueschel via R Seely)*

A smaller transport, yet one that was highly versatile for military duties was this Tachikawa Ki-54 "Hickory". These twin-engine aircraft not only served as light transports, normally carrying eight passengers, but as advanced and operational crew trainers. This Chinese marked "Topsy" was photographed at Hangchow, China, 12 November 1945.

*(Campbell Archives)*

A transport in lesser quantity in China was the Japanese Nakajima Ki-34 "Thora". Highly serviceable, they were designed in 1936 as the AT-2 for commercial service. Nearly 300 were produced for Japanese Army service as the Ki-34. This "Thora" was photographed at Peking (Beijing), China 17 November 1945. *(P Bowers via R Seely)*

### The French Air Force

As the war with Japan ended, what was then known as French Indo-China in South-east Asia, was quickly re-occupied by the French Army, beginning in August 1945. The French were soon faced with a rising Viet insurgency well-established within their former colony, yet had few aircraft on hand to quell disturbances. Their Armee de l'Air consisted of only three squadrons, two of which were war-weary transport aircraft and the third consisted of various types of aircraft. Few, if any, were of a combat variety to dispel the threat of Communist infiltrations.

Fighter pilots were sent from France to meet this threat, but when they first arrived in Saigon on 25 November 1945, there were no fighter aircraft in the French inventories in Indochina. Spitfire IXs, purchased from Great Britain, were to be shipped from France, but they were not due before the next January. These pilots needed to retain their proficiency, yet there was nothing for them to fly.

The defeated Japanese forces had left behind many aircraft, most of them in poor condition or severely damaged. The French managed to have a number of them repaired, and flown with a margin of success. A small number of Nakajima Ki-43-II and III "Oscars" were in the country, but proved to be more troublesome than practical. After repairs, the first was flight-tested at Saigon by one of the French pilots. At the conclusion of this flight, he made the uncomplimentary remark that he much preferred the earlier Curtiss 75A Hawks of earlier nineteen-thirties over the "Oscar".

Despite this negative comparison with the "Oscars", the only aircraft available, six of them were flown to Phnom-Penh by the French Groupes de Chasse 1/7 pilots on 7 December 1945. The decision to equip this squadron and CG II/7 with the Japanese fighters, pending the availability of the first Spitfires, became an official action. As sound as this action seemed at the time, the move was marred by a series of accidents that followed, primarily caused by undercarriage difficulties. One or both would stick in the 'up' position, causing major structural damage upon landing. By the first day of the New Year, 1946, only eight "Oscars" were operational. Mishaps continued in the form of mechanical problems. One by one they became damaged beyond economical repair whereby the last two "Oscars" were removed from squadron service on 7 February and were flown to the scrap yard.

"Oscars" were not the only Japanese aircraft used by the French in Indochina. Aichi E13A1 "Jakes" were used mainly for medical evacuation by the French Navy unit, Escadrille 8S, which had four in their inventory along with other aircraft types. One Mitsubishi Ki-46 "Dinah" was reported in French service as well. This fast, twin-engined aircraft was used for communications duties and occasionally as a VIP transport. As newer equipment began to arrive, along with their respective parts supply systems, the Japanese aircraft were soon, and willingly, phased out of French service in Indochina.

### Royal Thai Air Force

On the same day that the Japanese made their attack on the US Naval base at Pearl Harbor, Hawaii, on 7 December 1941, they also began their invasion of Thailand. Initially, the Thais resisted desperately, but seeing that they were fighting against odds not in their favour, they capitulated and became a satellite nation of the Japanese. The Royal Thai Air Force structure remained intact and became a co-belligerent force against the Allies, growing in strength and stature as the war progressed. In order to maintain this satellite air force, a number of Thai pilots were trained in Japan during the war at Army and Navy flight schools. As their numbers grew, they returned to Thailand, bringing back Nakajima Ki-43 "Oscars" and Mitsubishi A6M2 and A6M5 Zero fighters for their Royal Thai Air Force.

Other Japanese aircraft joined this growing fleet, which included Mitsubishi Ki-30 "Ann" light bombers, Mansyu Ki-79 two-seat advanced trainers and an assortment of Japanese-made gliders. The Royal Thai Navy also possessed a small air arm which was used for training and anti-submarine patrols. Included in this service were an unspecified number of Mitsubishi F1M2 two-seat "Pete" reconnaissance seaplanes, one of the rare biplane aircraft to survive the war years to remain in active service.

Experienced with Japanese aircraft during the war, it was not difficult for the Thais to continue their use of these and former Japanese-manned aircraft left behind by the departing Japanese after the surrender in 1945. Aside from various types, such as the Tachikawa Ki-55 Advanced Trainer "Ida", the additional numbers of Nakajima Ki-43 "Oscars" seems to have remained the most predominant Japanese aircraft in the Thai Air Force. Within a few days of the surrender, what Japanese "Oscars" still remained entered Royal Thai squadron service. Most were in natural metal, with the wartime Japanese Hinomaru painted over with the Thai insignia on the fuselage sides, leaving, in many instances, the Hinomaru on the top surface of their wings. These fighters and other Japanese aircraft remained in first-line service until about 1949 when attrition, and obsolescence, made it necessary to obtain replacements with more modern British and American types.

This Tachikawa Ki-36 "Ida" served the Japanese as a Direct Co-operation Plane in support of Army ground forces. The Thai's accepted them for the same purposes but served in their needs as a liaison and advanced trainer aircraft.
*(R Bueschel via R Seely)*

Thai pilots discuss air tactics under the wing of a Ki-43 "Oscar". Japanese aircraft stayed in Thai service for only a short time until resupplied with American aircraft and the much needed supply system for aircraft support. *(Koku Asahi via R Seely)*

This mix of newly-acquired Japanese aircraft residing in this hangar at Don Muang Airport, Bangkok, were made part of the Royal Thai Air Force. Seen here in September 1945 is a Mitsubishi Ki-30 "Ann" (centre), Tachikawa Ki-9 "Spruce" trainers, Vought SU Corsair (right) and at left is a Ki-43 "Oscar".
*(C Church via R Seely)*

Another country able to put the obsolete but available Japanese Mitsubishi Ki-30 "Ann" to operational duty was that of Thailand. Many of these light bombers were in that country when the war ended. The Royal Thai Air Force utilized these aircraft until replacements with American equipment began arriving in 1947. *(R Seely)*

### *Indonesian Air Force*

Other newly-liberated parts of Asia also fell heir to Japanese aircraft at the time of surrender. The islands of pre-war Netherlands East Indies, including Java and Sumatra, were another one of these examples. In their struggle to attain their independence from the Dutch, the newly-formed Indonesian People's Security Force, a nationalistic outgrowth of an underground group, opposed renewed Dutch control. Four years were to pass before the Netherlands accepted the inevitability of colonial independence, and it was during this initial four-year period of its existence that the Indonesian Air Force found itself in combat with Allied and Dutch forces.

This liberation force was well armed with confiscated Japanese stocks. They had also captured a number of assorted Japanese aircraft in the vicinity of Surabaya and Yogyakarta. For the most part, these were little more than piled scrap, but from the assorted parts, aircraft painstakingly came back to life. Among the first to fly was a Yokosuka K5Y1 "Willow" trainer, flown for the first time on 27 October 1945 from Tajikmalaya. Another aircraft credited by some sources as the first to fly on 10 October 1945, was a Mansyu Ki-97b, rebuilt from salvaged parts taken from an aircraft scrap yard at Djakarta. Both were used immediately as trainers for the new air arm.

From these men and machines was created the Air Force of the Indonesian Republic (*Angkatan Udara Republik Indonesia* or AURI). For this new air force, the Indonesian insignia simply comprised painting white over the lower half of the Japanese Hinomaru (Rising Sun). In other cases, a rectangle, similarly divided horizontally with red above and white below, replaced the disc.

Only a few Nakajima Ki-43 "Oscar" fighters remained in Indonesia, but these aircraft became the fighter strength of the newly-formed air force. The insurgent force continued to increase their aircraft stocks from the wrecks found in the former Japanese Army Air Force dumps. Additional "Oscars", probably belonging to the JAAF 33rd Sentai stationed at Medan in the Indies when the war ended, also served with the Indonesian forces from 1946 to 1949.

A token bomber force for the air arm of the Indonesian People's Security Force centred around a rebuilt Kawasaki Ki-48 "Lily" created from parts left behind by the Japanese. This twin-engine light bomber was used for some time until it was replaced by more modern aircraft. Another source suggests that a Nakajima Ki-49 Donryu "Helen" bomber was also incorporated into this air force. Eventually, this force comprised about fifty ex-Japanese aircraft in flying condition. By 1947, attrition had rendered nearly all to be unserviceable. At some unspecified time during that period, the following inventory of Japanese aircraft was operated by the Indonesian rebels:

  1 Kawanishi H6K5 "Mavis" Flying-boat
  1 Kawasaki Ki-48 "Lily" Light bomber
  1 Mitsubishi Ki-21 "Sally" Bomber
  4 Mitsubishi Ki-46 "Dinah" Reconnaissance
  6 Nakajima Ki-43 "Oscar" Fighter
  4 Tachikawa Ki-9 "Spruce" Trainer
  4 Tachikawa Ki-36 "Ida" Direct Co-operation
70 Yokosuka K5Y1 "Willow" Trainer
Source for inventory: *Air Wars and Aircraft,* by Victor Flintham, Facts on File, New York, 1990.

Part of the bomber force for the new Indonesian Air Force was this Mitsubishi Ki-51 "Sonia". Their fixed undercarriage made them obsolete by WW II standards, but these rugged aircraft served well to the end of the war in the ground support role for which they were designed. White painted over the lower half of the Japanese Hinomaru achieved the new Indonesian insignia. *(W Green via R Seely)*

A standard advanced single-engine trainer that the Japanese Army Air Force had throughout its area of service operations was this Tachikawa Ki-55 "Ida". The Indonesian Air Force put these to good use in the training of their own pilots. *(R Bueschel via R Seely)*

The Indonesian Air Force acquired several Yokosuka K5Y "Willow" biplane trainers for pilot training in their own air force. It is likely that the Japanese had these trainers in Indonesia for support flying between various air units as well as proficiency flying.

*(R Bueschel via R Seely)*

South Korea impressed this Tachikawa Ki-9 "Spruce" basic trainer into their own fledgling service. Time period would be about 1949/50 because of the insignia without a bar. Aircraft of this type were used for any number of flying type missions in addition to flight training.

*(B Reed via R Seely)*

Valuable Japanese aircraft to the Indonesians were flying boats such as this Kawanishi H6K5 "Mavis". They were ideal for reaching the outlying islands and remote shore locations of their new-forming country after the Pacific War. These aircraft were obsolete at the beginning of the Pacific War but many remained in service until the very end. This "Mavis" is believed to have been the only one of its type in Indonesian service.

*(P Selinger via R Seely)*

Former Japanese aircraft were reclaimed from scrap-heaps in Djakarta at the end of the war to serve the cause of Indonesian insurgents to obtain their independence from the Dutch. Here is a Nakajima Ki-43 "Oscar" as a fighter-bomber that was rebuilt from many parts and now carries new markings of the Indonesian Air Force.

*(W Green via R Seely)*

(1)  Mitsubishi A6M2 "Zeke" of the Australian War Memorial in Canberra, with the early Pacific War markings of the Tainan Kokutai carrying original tail code of V-173. It was recovered from the New Britain jungles around 1972 and restoration was accomplished at RAAF Base Wagga Wagga, NSW.

*(M Clayton)*

(9)  After years in a school yard (shown here), this Tachikawa Ki-54 "Hickory" fuselage is now in the hands of the RAAF Museum in Australia. It had carried the Japanese surrender delegation to Labuan, Borneo, in September 1945, and was later flown to Australia by RAAF crews. *(M Clayton)*

# CHAPTER IX
# REMAINING TREASURES

## Survivors of the Once Mighty Airpower

For many years, the number of surviving Japanese aircraft in the care of museums and individuals remained fairly constant. There was little interest in the few survivors with the exception of those particularly interested in this line of World War II aircraft. Beginning in the 1980s, there came a resurgence of interest in Japanese aircraft, both in museums as well as for individual collectors. The only new source for these aircraft were the jungles of the South-west Pacific Islands over which the air duels of the Pacific War were fought. Interested people made excursions into these parts of the world, only to be disappointed to find that corrosion had taken its toll. Where some of these aircraft were found in fairly reasonable condition, local governments prevented their removal for various reasons.

In time, however, these restrictions became more relaxed to those willing to pay for their removal, both to respective governments and to the work process. Slowly, from various reaches of that one-time expansive war zone, some of these hulks of Japanese aircraft have been recovered. Of these, some have been placed into restoration shops where they have been re-worked into reasonable condition in order to represent what they were once long ago. More are sure to come from the jungles and inconspicuous places where their presence were heretofore unknown or previously inaccessible.

(13) Only in recent years has the fuselage of this Tachikawa Ki-54a "Hickory" been revealed at the Beijing Aviation Museum, China. Aircraft of this type served as twin-engine advanced pilot trainers, crew trainers, and light transports.

*(S Uchibori via D Aiken)*

*Numbers in parenthesis at the start of the captions in this section cross reference to line entry number on lists that follow in this section.*

(16) Tachikawa Ki-55 advanced trainer "Ida" on outdoor exhibit in October 1980 at the People's Liberation Army Air Force Museum, Beijing. *(S Abe)*

One cannot forget, however, that this number of surviving Japanese aircraft is very small when considering that 10,700 aircraft were in Japan at the end of the war, according to the US Strategic Bombing Survey, *Japanese Air Power*. The reason that they met the destructive fate in the disarmament of Japan is understandable.

Many readers will remember certain Japanese aircraft that survived into the 1950s and 1960s in various locations, only to be eventually scrapped and destroyed because of neglect. This book was not intended to provide an accounting for each of these aircraft although each would have an interesting story to tell, only to have a sad ending.

To enable people having an interest in studying the survivors of that war that remain, a directory of these aircraft follows. At first glance this list will appear extensive, numbering 105 entries. In reality, however, when reviewing the condition of some, about thirty per cent may well be considered as derelicts, having some possibilities of restoration. In the meantime, however, these items can be useful for interpretation when investigating Japan's aviation technology. For that reason they have been listed here. About fifty examples of assembled and exhibitable aircraft can be regarded as true examples of their respective aircraft types (condition A). Surviving aircraft, having all their major components and in most cases not assembled but needing restoration to represent their original configurations, number about twenty-six examples (condition B). These two categories combine to roughly seventy-six aircraft, a figure fairly accurate as to what remains in the world at this writing that documents the technology of Japan's aviation. These aircraft represent about thirty different types used during the Pacific War.

This directory is in three parts, the first is a list by museum location that records the museum or owners having Japanese aircraft and identifies their holdings. A second part in this chapter is a repeat listing of these aircraft for those searching for aircraft by manufacturer and aircraft type. This list gives a more comprehensive overview of the types and numbers of Japanese aircraft that do survive, and regrettably provides the evidence – or lack thereof – that gives an indication of the many aircraft types that no longer exist. A sampling of photographs concludes this chapter which pictorially shows the current status of many of these aircraft. The number in parenthesis keys that photograph to the entries found in the two listings.

EXISTING JAPANESE AIRCRAFT
Listed by country location
(As of late-1991)

Condition Code:
A – Complete and exhibitable aircraft.
B – All basic components and not assembled.
C – Some basic components or needs major restoration.
F – Flyable.
R – Replica.
* – Serial number suspect.

| Museum and Aircraft Type | Other Mark | Serial | Condition |
|---|---|---|---|
| **AUSTRALIA** | | | |
| Australian War Memorial | | | |
| P.O. Box 305, Canberra City, A.C.T. 2601 | | | |
| (1)  Mitsubishi A6M2 "Zeke" | V-173 | Mit 5784 | A |
| (Found at Gasmata, N Britain) | | | |
| (2)  Mitsubishi A6M2 "Zeke" | | Mit 3618 | C |
| (Found at Kahili, Bouganville) | | | |
| (3)  Mitsubishi A6M5 "Zeke" | 3-108 | Mit 4043 | C |
| (On New Britian until 1972) | | | |
| (4)  Nakajima Ki-43-I "Oscar" | | 4700 * | C |
| (5)  Nakajima Ki-43-I "Oscar" | | 6023 * | C |
| (6)  Nakajima Ki-43-II "Oscar" (fuse. and eng.) | | | C |
| (7)  Nakajima Ki-43-II "Oscar" | | 5465 | C |
| | | | |
| Mr. Colin Pay | | | |
| Pay's Air Service | | | |
| Scone Aerodrome, Scone, NSW 2337 | | | |
| (8)  Nakajima Ki-43-I Hei "Oscar" | | 650 or 750 | B |
| | | | |
| Royal Australian Air Force Museum | | | |
| RAAF Base, Point Cook, Victoria 3029 | | | |
| (9)  Tachikawa Ki-54 "Hickory" (fuselage only) | | | C |
| (At RAAF Fairbairn until 1980) | | | |
| | | | |
| Darwin Aviation Museum | | | |
| P.O. Box 38037, Winnellie NT 0821 | | | |
| (10)  Mitsubishi A6M2 "Zeke" | BII-124 | Mit 5349 | C |
| (From Melville Is, Aust.) | | | |
| (11)  Mitsubishi G4M "Betty" | | | C |
| | | | |
| **CANADA** | | | |
| Diemert (Robert) | | | |
| Carmen, Manitoba | | | |
| (12)  Mitsubishi A6M5 "Zeke" | | | C |
| (From Ballale, Solomon Is.) | | | |
| | | | |
| **CHINA** | | | |
| Beijing Aviation Museum | | | |
| 37 Xue Yuan Road, Beijing Aeronautical Institute, Beijing 1000083 | | | |
| (13)  Tachikawa Ki-54a "Hickory" (fuselage) | | | C |
| | | | |
| Military Museum of the Chinese People's Revolution | | | |
| 9 Fuxing Lu,, Beijing | | | |
| (14)  Mitsubishi A6M5 "Zeke" | | | B |

People's Liberation Army Air Force Museum
Datang Shan, Changping, Beijing 102211
| | | | |
|---|---|---|---|
| (15) | Kawasaki Ki-48 "Lily" (fuselage only) | | C |
| (16) | Tachikawa Ki-55 "Ida" | 02 | A |

**ENGLAND**
Aerospace Museum
Royal Air Force, Cosford, Shifnal, Shropshire TF11 8UP
| | | | | |
|---|---|---|---|---|
| (17) | Kawasaki Ki-100-I Otsu | | 16336 | A |
| (18) | Yokosuka Ohka 11   BAPC.99, | RAF#8486M | | A |
| (19) | Mitsubishi Ki-46-III "Dinah" | | 5439 | A |

Defence EOD School
Lodge Hill Camp, Chattenden, Rochester, Kent ME3 8NZ
| | | |
|---|---|---|
| (20) | Yokosuka Ohka 11   BAPC.159 | A |

Fleet Air Arm Museum
Royal Naval Air Station, Yeovilton, Ilchester, Somerset BA22 8HT
| | | |
|---|---|---|
| (21) | Yokosuka Ohka 1   BAPC.58 | A |
| | (Science Museum ownership) | |

Greater Manchester Museum of Science and Industry
Liverpool Road, Castlefield, Manchester M3 4JP
| | | |
|---|---|---|
| (22) | Yokosuka Ohka 11   BAPC.98, RAF#8485M | A |
| | (RAF Museum ownership) | |

Imperial War Museum
Lambeth Road, London SE1 6HZ
| | | | |
|---|---|---|---|
| (23) | Mitsubishi A6M5 (Cockpit) | BI-05 | C |

**INDIA**
Indian Air Museum
Palam Air Station, Delhi 10
| | | |
|---|---|---|
| (24) | Yokosuka Ohka 11 | A |

**INDONESIA**
Museum Pusat Tni-Au
Dirgantara Mandala, Lanud Adisutjipto, Yogyakarta 55002
| | | | |
|---|---|---|---|
| (25) | Mitsubishi A6M5 "Zeke" | 30-1153 | A |
| (26) | Mitsubishi Ki-51 "Sonia" | G32 | A |
| (27) | Nakajima Ki-43-II "Oscar" | H45 | A |

Museum Abri Satriamandala
Jalan Gatot Dubroto 14, Jakarta - Selantan, Java
| | | | |
|---|---|---|---|
| (28) | Yokosuka K5Y "Willow" | 62 TJ | A |
| (29) | Mansyu Ki-79b Trainer | | A |

**JAPAN**
Air And Space Museum
Nagoya Airport Building, Toyoyama-cho
Nishikasugai-gun, Aichi Prefecture 480-02
| | | | |
|---|---|---|---|
| (30) | Mitsubishi A6M3 Model 32 | Y2-128 | A |
| | (From Majiro, Marshall Is.) | | |

Gifu Air Base Collection
Naka, Kakamigahara City, Gifu Prefecture 504
| | | |
|---|---|---|
| (31) | Aichi E13A1 "Jake" | C |
| (32) | Mitsubishi J8M1 Shusui (Fuselage) | C |

Hamamatsu Air Base Collection, O, Nishiyama-chou, Hamamatsu-cho, Shizuoka Prefecture 432
(33)    Mitsubishi A6M5 "Zeke"                43-188            Mit 4685              A
        (From Guam, 1963)

Iruma Air Base, Saitama Prefecture
(34)    Yokosuka Ohka 11                                                            A

Kamikaze Museum, P.O. Box 897-03, Chiran, Kagoshima Prefecture
(35)    Kawasaki Ki-61-IIkai "Tony"                          5070                   A
        (Formerly at Kawaguchiko and Yokota AB)
(36)    Mitsubishi A6M7 "Zeke" (Recovered shell, exhibit)            C

Harada, Nobuo, 3-16-11 Kugahara, Ohta, Tokyo  (Formerly:Kawaguchiko Motor Museum)
(37)    Mitsubishi A6M2 "Zeke"                              Naka 91518             C
(38)    Mitsubishi A6M2 "Zeke"                              Naka 92717 *           C
(39)    Mitsubishi A6M5 "Zeke"                              Mit 4241               A
(40)    Mitsubishi A6M5 "Zeke"                              1493 *                 C
(41)    Mitsubishi G4M2 "Betty" (aft fuselage only)                                C
(42)    Yokosuka K5Y1 "Willow"(Replica)                                            R

Kyoto-Arashiyama Museum, 32-22 Tsukurimuchi-cho, Sagatenryu-ji, Ukyo-ku, Kyoto
(43)    Mitsubishi A6M7 "Zeke 63"            210-118B                              A
(44)    Nakajima Ki-84-1-Ko "Frank"          ATIU S-17)        1446                A

Leisure Land, Ehime Prefecture, Shikoku
(45)    Kawanishi N1K2-J "George"                                                  C

Museum of Maritime Science, 3-1 Higashi-Yashio, Shinagawa-ku, Tokyo 135
(46)    Kawanishi H8K2 "Emily"                               426                   A

National Science Museum, 7-20 Ueno-Koen, Taito-ku, Tokyo 110
(47)    Mitsubishi A6M2 (2-seat) "Zeke"      53-122                                A
        (From 253 Kokutai)

Yasukuni Jinja Yushukan, 1-1 Kudan-Kita 3 Chome, Chiyoda-ku, Tokyo 102
(48)    Yokosuka D4Y1 "Judy"                 "Taka"-13         4316                A
        (From Yap, Caroline Is.)
(49)    Yokosuka MXY7 Ohka 11 (Replica)                                            R

Zero Hangar Visitor Center, Marine Corps Air Station, Iwakuni, Yamaguchi Prefecture
(50)    Mitsubishi A6M5 "Zeke" (Replica)                                           R

Mitsubishi Heavy Industry, Komaki South Plant, Nagoya
(51)    Mitsubishi A6M5a "Zeke"                              Mit 4708              A

National Self-Defense Air Force's Air Museum, Kagamihara City, Gifu Prefecture
(52)    Nakajima Ki-115 Tsurugi (See page 128)                                     B

**NEW IRELAND**
Maimaluau
(53)    Mitsubishi A6M2 "Zeke"                                                     B

**NEW ZEALAND**
Auckland Institute and Museum
The Domain, Parnell, Auckland
(54)    Mitsubishi A6M3 Model 22             2-182             Mit 3844             A

**PAPUA NEW GUINEA**
Coastwatchers War Memorial

Rabaul, New Britain
(55)    Mitsubishi A6M5 "Zeke"                                                              B

National Museum and Art Gallery
of Papua New Guinea
(56)    Kawasaki Ki-61-Ib "Tony"                                    640                     C

**THAILAND**
Royal Thai Air Force Museum
Don Muang Air Force Base, Bangkok 10210
(57)    Tachikawa Ki-24 Primary Glider                                                     A
(58)    Tachikawa Ki-24 Primary Glider                                                     B
(59)    Tachikawa Ki-36 "Ida"                                                              A

**UNITED STATES**
Admiral Nimitz Center
Fredericksburg, Texas 78624
(60)    Aichi D3A2 "Val"                                            3105                    C
        (From Gasmata, New Britain)
(61)    Kawanishi N1K1 "Rex"                                        562                     A
        (US Navy ownership)

Air Force Museum
Wright Patterson AFB, Dayton, Ohio 45433
(62)    Kawanishi N1K2-J "George"          343-A-11               5312                     A
(63)    Mitsubishi A6M2 "Zeke"                           Naka 51553                        B
        (Under restoration)
(64)    Yokosuka MXY7-K1 (Ohka 11 Trainer)                                                 A

R. D. Wittington
1020 N.W. 62nd Street, Ft. Lauderdale, Florida 33309
(65)    Mitsubishi A6M5 "Zeke"                                      5350                    B
        (From Saipan, 1944 and Atlanta Museum in 1991)

Confederate Air Force
Midland International Airport, Midland, Texas 79711
(66)    Mitsubishi A6M2 "Zeke"             EII-102        Naka 5356 *                       F
        (From Ballale Is. via Robt Diemert))

EAA Museum
Wittman Airfield, Oshkosh, Wisconsin 54903-2591
(67)    Nakajima Ki-43-IIb "Oscar"                                  6430                    A
        (NASM ownership)

Marine Corps Air Ground Museum
Quantico Marine Base, Building 2014
Quantico, Virginia 22134
(68)    Yokosuka Ohka 11                                            1018                    A

Museum of Flying, 2772 Donald Douglas Loop N., Santa Monica, California 90405
(69)    Kawasaki Ki-61 Hien "Tony"                                                          C
(70)    Mitsubishi A6M3 Model  22 "Zeke"                                                    C
(102)   Mitsubishi A6M "Zeke"                                                               C
(103)   Mitsubishi A6M "Zeke"                                                               C
(71)    Mitsubishi G4M1 "Betty"                                                             C
(72)    Yokosuka D4Y Suisei "Judy"                                                          C

National Air and Space Museum (NASM), Smithsonian Institution, Washington, DC 20560
(73)    Aichi B7A2 "Grace"                                          816                     B

| | | | | |
|---|---|---|---|---|
| (74) | Aichi M6A1 Seiran | | 1600228 | B |
| (75) | Kawanishi N1K1 "Rex" | | 514 | B |
| (76) | Kawanishi N1K2-J "George" | | 5341 | B |
| (77) | Kawasaki Ki-45kai "Nick" | T2-701 | 4268 | B |
| (78) | Kyushu J7W1 Shinden | T2-326 | | B |
| (79) | Mitsubishi A6M5 "Zeke" | T2-130 | Mit 4340 | A |
| (80) | Mitsubishi G4M3 "Betty" (Nose & tail cones) | | C | |
| (81) | Nakajima B6N2 "Jill" | | 5350 | B |
| (82) | Nakajima C6N1-S "Myrt" | T2-N4803 | 4161 | B |
| (83) | Nakajima J1N1-S "Irving" | T2-N700 | 7334 | A |
| (84) | Nakajima Kikka | | 7337* | B |
| (85) | Nakajima Ki-115 Tsurugi | T2-556 | 1002 | B |
| (86) | Yokosuka Ohka 22 (Modif. to Ohka 11) | | | A |
| (87) | Yokosuka MXY7-K2 (Ohka 2-seat Trainer) | | 61 | C |
| (88) | Yokosuka P1Y1-S "Frances" | T2-1702 | 8923 | B |

National Museum of Naval Aviation, US Naval Air Station, Pensacola, Florida 32508

| | | | | |
|---|---|---|---|---|
| (89) | Mitsubishi A6M2 "Zeke" | EII-140 | Naka 5450* | A |
| | (Formerly at Liberal and USMC Museums, from Ballale Is, via Robt. Diemert) | | | |

Naval Memorial Museum, Washington Navy Yard, Building 76, Washington, DC 20374

| | | | | |
|---|---|---|---|---|
| (90) | Yokosuka MXY7-K1 (Ohka 11 Trainer) | | 5100 | A |

New England Air Museum, Bradley International Airport, Windsor Locks, Connecticut 06096

| | | | | |
|---|---|---|---|---|
| (91) | Kawanishi N1K2-J "George" | | 5128 | B |
| | (US Navy ownership) | | | |

Planes of Fame, Chino Airport, 7000 Merrill Ave, Chino, California 91710

| | | | | |
|---|---|---|---|---|
| (92) | Aichi D3A2 "Val" | | 3178 | A |
| | (From Ballale Is, via Robt. Diemert) | | | |
| (93) | Yokosuka Ohka 11 | | 1049 | A |
| (94) | Mitsubishi A6M5 "Zeke" | 61-120 | Naka 5357 | F |
| (95) | Mitsubishi A6M5 "Zeke" | HK-102 | Mit 4400 | A |
| (96) | Mitsubishi J2M3 "Jack" | | 3014 | A |
| (97) | Mitsubishi J8M1 Shusui | | 403 | A |

San Diego Aerospace Museum
2001 Pan American Plaza, Balboa Park, San Diego, California 92101

| | | | | |
|---|---|---|---|---|
| (98) | Mitsubishi A6M7 "Zeke" | | Naka 23186 | A |
| | (NASM ownership) | | | |

Sterling, John & Tom
1081 N Mitchell, Boise, Idaho  83704

| | | | | |
|---|---|---|---|---|
| (99) | Mitsubishi A6M3 Model 22 | Y2-176 | Mit 3685 | C |
| | (252nd Kokutai) | | | |
| (100) | Mitsubishi A6M3 Model 32 | S-1128 | Mit 3318 | C |
| | (Chitose Kokutai) | | | |
| | (Both from Taroa, Marshall Is.) | | | |

Weeks Air Museum
14710 SW 128th Street, Miami, Florida 33186

| | | | | |
|---|---|---|---|---|
| (101) | Kawasaki Ki-61-I "Tony" | (78th Sentai) | 379 | C |
| | (From Wewak, Papua New Guinea) | | | |
| (2) | Mitsubishi A6M2 "Zeke" | | Mit 3618 | C |
| | (From Australian War Memorial, parts only) | | | |
| (3) | Mitsubishi A6M5 "Zeke" | 3-108 | Mit 4043 | C |
| | (From Australian War Memorial) | | | |

Willow Grove Naval Air Station
Willow Grove, Pennsylvania 19090
(104)   Kawanishi N1K1 "Rex"                                      565            A

Yankee Air Corps
Chino Airport, Chino, California 91710
(105)   Yokosuka Ohka 11                                                        A

(18) Among other missiles at the Aerospace Museum, Cosford, England, is this suspended Yokosuka Ohka 11 kamikaze aircraft with the often used
I-13 number.

*(Birmingham Evening Mail)*

# EXISTING JAPANESE AIRCRAFT
## Listed by Aircraft Manufacturer
### (As of Late-1991)

Condition Code:
A – Complete and exhibitable aircraft.
B – All basic components and not assembled.
C – Some basic components or needing major restoration.
F – Flyable.
R – Replica.
* – Serial number suspect.

| Mfg. and Type | Other Mark | Serial | Location | Condition |
|---|---|---|---|---|
| **AICHI** | | | | |
| (73) B7A1 Ryusei "Grace" | | 816 | NASM, Garber Fac., Washington, DC, USA | B |
| (92) D3A2 Type 99 CB "Val" | | 3178 | Planes of Fame, Chino, California, USA | A |
| (60) D3A2 Type 99 CB "Val" | | 3105 | Adm. Nimitz Museum, Fredericksburg, TX | C |
| (31) E13A1 Reconn SP "Jake" | | | Gifu AB, Gifu Prefecture, Japan | C |
| (74) M6A1 Serian Spl Attack | | 1600228 | NASM, Garber Fac., Washington, DC, USA | B |
| | | | | |
| **KAWANISHI** | | | | |
| (73) H8K2 Type 2 FB "Emily" | | 426 | Museum of Maritime Science, Tokyo, Japan | A |
| (75) N1K1 Kyofu "Rex" | | 514 | NASM, Garber Fac., Washington, DC, USA | B |
| (61) N1K1 Kyofu "Rex" | | 562 | Adm. Nimitz Museum, Fredericksburg, TX | A |
| (104) N1K1 Kyofu "Rex" | | 565 | NAS Willow Grove, Pennsylvania, USA | A |
| (76) N1K2-J Shiden-Kai "George" | | 5341 | NASM, Garber Fac., Washington, DC, USA | B |
| (91) N1K2-J Shiden-Kai "George" | | 5128 | New England Air Museum, Conn., USA | B |
| (62) N1K2-J Shiden-Kai "George" | | 5312 | US Air Force Museum, Dayton, Ohio, USA | A |
| (45) N1K2-J Shiden-Kai "George" | | | Leisure Land, Ehime, Shikoku, Japan | C |
| | | | | |
| **KAWASAKI** | | | | |
| (77) Ki-45kai Toryu "Nick" | | 4268 | NASM, Garber Fac., Washington, DC, USA | B |
| (15) Ki-48 Type 99 LB "Lily" (Fuse) | | | People's Liberation AAF Museum, China | C |
| (69) Ki-61 Hien "Tony" | | | Museum of Flying, Santa Monica, CA, USA | C |
| (101) Ki-61-I Hien "Tony" | | 379 | Weeks Air Museum, Miami, Florida, USA | C |
| (56) Ki-61-Ib Hien "Tony" | | 640 | National Museum, Papua New Guinea | C |
| (35) Ki-61-IIkai Hien "Tony" | | 5070 | Kamikaze Museum, Chiran, Kyushu, Japan | A |
| (17) Ki-100-I Otsu,  BAPC 83 | | 16336 | Aerospace Museum, RAF, Cosford, England | A |
| | | | | |
| **KUGISHO (See YOKOSUKA)** | | | | |
| | | | | |
| **KYUSHU** | | | | |
| (78) J7W1 Shinden | T2-326 | | NASM, Garber Fac., Washington, DC, USA | B |
| | | | | |
| **MANSYU** | | | | |
| (29) Ki-79b Trainer | | | Museum Abri Satriamandala, Indonesia | A |
| | | | | |
| **MITSUBISHI** | | | | |
| (66) A6M2 Reisen "Zeke" | EII-102 | 5356* | Confederate Air Force, Texas, USA | F |
| (89) A6M2 Reisen "Zeke" | EII-140 | 5450* | Natl Museum of Naval Aviation, FL, USA | A |

| | | | | |
|---|---|---|---|---|
| (1) A6M2 Reisen "Zeke" | | 5784 | Australian War Memorial, Canberra, Aust. | A |
| (63) A6M2 Reisen "Zeke" | | 51553 | US Air Force Museum, Dayton, Ohio, USA | B |
| (37) A6M2 Reisen "Zeke" | | 91518 | Harada (Nobuo), Ohta, Tokyo, Japan | C |
| (38) A6M2 Reisen "Zeke" | | 92717* | Harada (Nobuo),Ohta, Tokyo, Japan | C |
| (47) A6M2 Reisen "Zeke" | 53-122 | | Tokyo Science Museum, Ueno Park, Japan | A |
| (53) A6M2 Reisen "Zeke" | | | Maimaluau, New Ireland | B |
| (10) A6M2 Reisen "Zeke" | BII-124 | 5349 | Darwin Aviation Museum, Winnellie, Aust. | C |
| (100) A6M3 Reisen "ZeKe" | S-1128 | 3318 | Sterling (John/Tom), Boise, Idaho, USA | C |
| (2) A6M3 Model 22 "Zeke" | | 3618 | Australian War Memorial, Canberra, Aust. | C |
| (99) A6M3 Model 22 "Zeke" | Y2-176 | 3685 | Sterling (John/Tom), Boise, Idaho, USA | C |
| (54) A6M3 Model 22 "Zeke" | 2-182 | 3844 | Auckland Inst. and Museum, New Zealand | A |
| (70) A6M3 Model 22 "Zeke" | | | Museum of Flying, Santa Monica, CA, USA | C |
| (30) A6M3 Model 32 "Zeke" | Y2-128 | | Nagoya Airport Building, Japan | A |
| (102) A6M  Reisen "Zeke" | | | Museum of Flying, Santa Monica, CA, USA | C |
| (103) A6M  Reisen "Zeke" | | | Museum of Flying, Santa Monica, CA, USA | C |
| (25) A6M5 Reisen "Zeke" | 30-1153 | | Museum Pusat Tni-Au, Indonesia | A |
| (40) A6M5 Reisen "Zeke" | | 1493* | Harada (Nobuo),  Ohta, Tokyo, Japan | C |
| (3) A6M5 Reisen "Zeke" | 3-108 | 4043 | Weeks Air Museum, Miami, Florida, USA | C |
| (39) A6M5 Reisen "Zeke" | | 4241 | Harada (Nobuo),  Ohta, Tokyo, Japan | A |
| (79) A6M5 Reisen "Zeke" | | 4340 | NASM, Smithsonian, Washington, DC, USA | A |
| (95) A6M5 Reisen "Zeke" | HK-102 | 4400* | Planes of Fame, Chino, California, USA | A |
| (33) A6M5 Reisen "Zeke" | 43-188 | 4685 | Hamamatsu AB Collection, Japan | A |
| (51) A6M5a Reisen "Zeke" | | 4708 | Mitsubishi Heavy Industry, Nagoya, Japan | A |
| (65) A6M5 Reisen "Zeke" | | 5350 | R. D. Wittington, Ft. Lauderdale, Florida, USA | B |
| (94) A6M5 Reisen "Zeke" | 61-120 | 5357 | Planes of Fame, Chino, California, USA | F |
| (23) A6M5 Reisen "Zeke" | BI-05 | | Imperial War Museum, London, England | C |
| (55) A6M5 Reisen "Zeke" | | | War Memorial, Rabaul, New Britain, PNG | B |
| (12) A6M2 Reisen "Zeke" | | | Diemert (Rob), Carmen, Manitoba, Canada | C |
| (14) A6M5 Reisen "Zeke" | | | Mil. Museum of Chinese People's Rev. | B |
| (50) A6M5 Reisen "Zeke" (Replica) | | | Zero Hangar, Iwakuni, Japan | R |
| (36) A6M7 Reisen "Zeke" | | | Kamikaze Museum, Chiran, Kago., Japan | C |
| (98) A6M7 Reisen "Zeke" | | 23186 | San Diego Aerospace Museum, CA (NASM's) | A |
| (43) A6M7 Reisen "Zeke" | 210-118B | | Kyoto-Arashiyama Museum, Japan | A |
| (71) G4M1 Type 1, "Betty" | | | Museum of Flying, Santa Monica, CA, USA | C |
| (11) G4M Type 1, "Betty" | | | Darwin Aviation Museum, Winnellie, Aust. | C |
| (41) G4M2 Type 1, "Betty" (Aft fuselage) | | | Harada (Nobuo), Ohta, Tokyo, Japan | C |
| (80) G4M3 Type 1, (Cockpit/tail cone) | | | NASM, Garber Fac., Washington, DC, USA | C |
| (96) J2M3 Raiden "Jack" | | 3014 | Planes of Fame, Chino, California, USA | A |
| (97) J8M1 Shusui | | 403 | Planes of Fame, Chino, California, USA | A |
| (32) J8M1 Shusui (Fuselage only) | | | Gifu AB, Gifu Prefecture, Japan | C |
| (19) Ki-46-III "Dinah",  BAPC 84 | | 5439 | Aerospace Museum, RAF, Cosford, England | A |
| (26) Ki-51 Type 99 LB "Sonia" | G32 | | Museum Pusat Tni-Au, Indonesia | A |

NAKAJIMA

| | | | | |
|---|---|---|---|---|
| (81) B6N2 Tenzan "Jill" | | 5350 | NASM, Garber Fac., Washington, DC, USA | B |
| (82) C6M1-S "Saiun "Myrt" | | 4161 | NASM, Garber Fac., Washington, DC, USA | B |
| (83) J1N1-S Gekko "Irving" | | 7334 | NASM, Garber Fac., Washington, DC, USA | A |
| (4) Ki-43-I Hayabusa "Oscar" | | 4700* | Australian War Memorial, Canberra, Aust. | C |
| (5) Ki-43-I Hayabusa "Oscar" | | 6023* | Australian War Memorial, Canberra, Aust. | C |

| | | | |
|---|---|---|---|
| (8) Ki-43-I Hei Hayabusa "Oscar" | 750 | Pay's Air Service, Scone, NSW, Australia | B |
| (27) Ki-43-II Hayabusa "Oscar" | H45 | Museum Pusat Tni-Au, Indonesia | A |
| (6) Ki-43-II Hayabusa "Oscar" (Fuse) | | Australian War Memorial, Canberra, Aust. | C |
| (7) Ki-43-II Hayabusa "Oscar" | 5465 | Australian War Memorial, Canberra, Aust. | C |
| (67) Ki-43-IIb Hayabusa "Oscar" | 6430 | EAA Museum, Oshkosh, WI, USA (NASM's) | A |
| (44) Ki-84 Hayate "Frank" | 1446 | Kyoto-Arashiyama Museum, Japan | A |
| (85) Ki-115 Tsurugi | 1002 | NASM, Garber Fac., Washington, DC, USA | B |
| (52) Ki-115 Tsurugi | | High school location in Tokyo, Japan | B |
| (84) Kikka | 7337* | NASM, Garber Fac., Washington, DC, USA | B |

### TACHIKAWA

| | | | |
|---|---|---|---|
| (57) Ki-24 Primary Glider | | Royal Thai Air Force Museum, Bangkok | A |
| (58) Ki-24 Primary Glider | | Royal Thai Air Force Museum, Bangkok | B |
| (9) Ki-54 "Hickory" (Fuselage only) | | RAAF Museum, Point Cook, Australia | C |
| (13) Ki-54a "Hickory" (Fuselage only) | | Beijing Aviation Museum, China | C |
| (16) Ki-55 "Ida" Trainer | 02 | People's Liberation AAF Museum, China | A |
| (59) Ki-36 "Ida" Direct Coop. | | Royal Thai Air Force Museum, Bangkok | A |

### YOKOSUKA

(Note:  For aircraft designed by the Kaigun Koku-Gijutsu-Sho, the more popular name Yokosuka has been used rather than the more correct acronym Kugisho.)

| | | | |
|---|---|---|---|
| (64) MXY7-K1 "Baka" | | US Air Force Museum, Dayton, Ohio, USA | A |
| (90) MXY7-K1 "Baka" | 5100 | Navy Memorial Museum, Washington, USA | A |
| (87) MXY7-K2 "Baka" | 61 | NASM, Garber Fac., Washington, DC, USA | C |
| (21) Ohka 11 "Baka"  BAPC 58 | | FAA Museum, Yeovilton, Somerset, England | A |
| (22) Ohka 11 "Baka"  BAPC 98 | | Gtr. Manchester Museum, Manchester, Eng. | A |
| (18) Ohka 11 "Baka"  BAPC 99RAF#8486M | | Aerospace Museum, RAF, Cosford, England | A |
| (20) Ohka 11 "Baka"  BAPC 159 | | Defence EOD School, Rochester, Kent, Eng | A |
| (24) Ohka 11 "Baka" | | Indian Air Museum, New Delhi, India | A |
| (34) Ohka 11 "Baka" | | Iruma AB, Saitama Prefecture, Japan | A |
| (49) Ohka 11 "Baka" (Replica) | | Yasukuni Jinja Yushukan, Tokyo, Japan | R |
| (68) Ohka 11 "Baka" | 1018 | USMC Air Ground Museum, Quantico, VA USA | A |
| (105) Ohka 11 "Baka" | | Yankee Air Corps, Chino, California, USA | A |
| (93) Ohka 11 "Baka" | 1049 | Planes of Fame, Chino, California, USA | A |
| (86) Ohka 22 "Baka" Mock-up to Ohka 11 | | NASM, Garber Fac., Washington, DC, USA | A |
| (48) D4Y1 "Judy"  "Taka"-13 | 4316 | Yasukuni Jinja Yushukan, Tokyo, Japan | A |
| (72) D4Y "Judy" | | Museum of Flying, Santa Monica, CA, USA | C |
| (28) K5Y1 "Willow" Trainer  62 TJ | | Museum Abri Satriamandala, Indonesia | A |
| (42) K5Y1 "Willow" Trainer (Replica) | | Harada, Noburo,  Ohta, Tokyo, Japan | R |
| (88) P1Y1-S Ginga "Frances" | 8923 | NASM, Garber Fac., Washington, DC, USA | B |

(15) Kawasaki Ki-48 "Lilys" once made up the bomber force of the post-war Chinese Nationalist Air Force. This forward section of a fuselage at the People's Liberation Army Air Force Museum in Beijing is all that remains for this aircraft type. These light bombers were a versatile aircraft for the Japanese Army throughout the entire Pacific War. *(B. Ogden)*

(17) Kawasaki Ki-100-Ib is the only survivor of its type. It is located at the Aerospace Museum, RAF Cosford, England, shown here on temporary outdoor exhibit. The engine operates and is run periodically. It is thought that this Ki-100 was sent to the UK from Malaya at the end of the war along with the "Dinah" at the same museum.

*(Aerospace Museum, Cosford)*

OKA-11

A Japanese Suicide Bomb flown by KAMAKASI pilots against
aircraft carriers in the pacific area during World War II. An early
guided bomb with manual guidance and control. OKA weighs 4718 lbs
of which 2461lb is warhead.
Released from a Mitsubishi G4-M2 bomber upto 50 miles from its target
OKAS moved with rocket assistance reached 534 m.p.h. The three Type 4
2 in 1 model 20 rockets each delivered 1763 lb thrust for eight to ten
seconds, and during final approach at an angle of 50° speed was 620mph.
The pilot crashed on the carrier and joined his ancestors.

(20) Suspended in the diving
attack mode is this Yokosuka
Ohka 11 "Baka Bomb" at the
Defence Explosive Ordnance
Disposal School at Lodge Hill
Camp, Chattenden, England.
Since this is a military facility,
it is not available for viewing
by the general public.

*(EOD School)*

(19)  A one of a kind survivor
is this Mitsubishi Ki-46-III
which now resides at the
Aerospace Museum, Cosford,
England. It is believed to have
been sent to England in
1945/46 from ATAIU-SEA,
RAF Tebrau, Johore, Malaya.
It is doubtful that it was flown
in the UK.

*(R Cranham)*

(21) Another one of four Ohka 11 "Baka Bombs" that reside in England is this one at the Fleet Air Arm Museum at Yeovilton. It is actually owned by the Science Museum.

*(FAA Museum)*

The Indian Air Museum located at the Palam Air Station, Delhi, India, displays this well-maintained Yokosuka Ohka 11 "Baka Bomb."

(23) All that remains of this A6M5 "Zeke" BI-05 that was captured and tested in Singapore is the cockpit and stub wing section. It now resides in the collection of the Imperial War Museum, London.

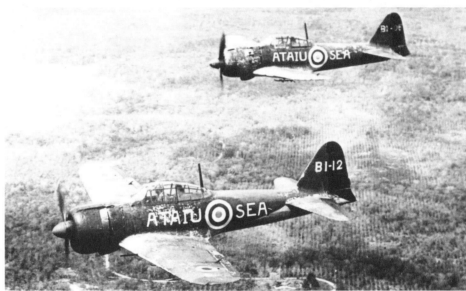

This photo shows this A6M5, BI-05, along with A6M2, BI-12 being flight evaluated near Singapore by BI (British Intelligence).

(33) This A6M5 Zero fighter found on Guam in 1962, was restored by JASDF Depot Maintenance personnel at Gifu AB and presented to Japan by the US on 3 November 1964. It now resides at Hamamatsu AB. It had been assigned to the 343rd Kokutai when it became a casualty in the "Marianas Turkey Shoot".

(25) The Museum Pusat Tni-Au in Indonesia maintains three Japanese aircraft in its fairly large yet slightly known collection at Yogyakarta. This Mitsubishi A6M5 is reported to be well maintained Since this collection is located on a military air base, it is not readily accessible to the public. *(B. Ogden)*

(27) A makeshift canopy alters the familiar lines of this Nakajima Ki-43-II "Oscar" that is part of the collection at the Museum Pusat Tni-Au, Yogyakarta, Indonesia. Fighters of this type were rebuilt from scrapped parts left behind by the Japanese at the end of the war. They comprised the main fighter strength for the Indonesian rebels when striving for their independence. *(B Ogden)*

(26) This Mitsubishi Ki-51 "Sonia" is a sole survivor of its type and resides in the Museum Pusat Tni-Au in Indonesia. Used as a light bomber by the Japanese Army, the few that were left abandoned in Java and Sumatra at the end of the war were briefly used against Dutch forces by the fledgling Indonesian Air Force. *(B. Ogden)*

(28) The standard basic trainer for the Japanese Navy was this Yokosuka K5Y1 "Willow". Now in the Museum Abri Satriamandala in Java, it carries Republic of Indonesia insignia as it did when it served the Indonesian People's Security Force. *(S Abe)*

(29) In outdoor exhibit is this Mansyu Ki-79b trainer at the Museum Abri Satriamandala, Jakarta, Java. This Japanese aircraft made from scrapped parts was the first to be flown by rebel forces that eventually formed an independent Indonesian Republic. *(S Abe)*

(33) This is all that remains of a rocket-powered Mitsubishi J8M1 Shusui, Japanese version of the Messerschmitt Me 163 fighter. Now at Gifu Air Base, it had been found in a cave at Yokosuka in the 1960s.

*(K Owaki)*

(30) This restored Mitsubishi A6M3 "Zeke 32" recovered from Tarawa Island in the Gilberts, resides at the Nagoya Airport Terminal Museum, Japan. It carries the unit marking Y2-128 of the 252nd Kokutai when operating from Tarawa .

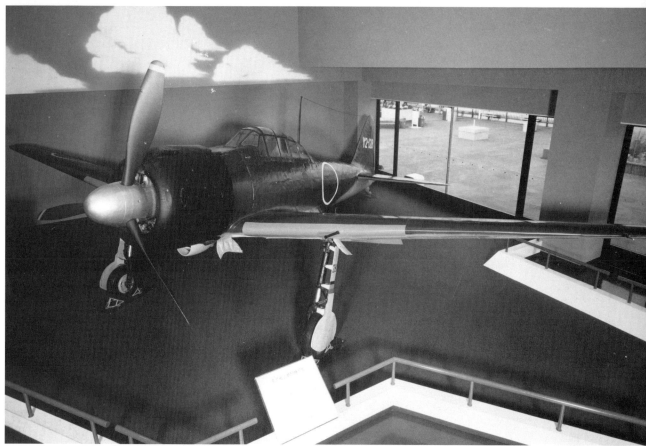

(35) This Kawasaki Ki-61 "Tony" is in the Kamikaze Museum, Kyushu. It is shown here in its third known marking scheme, now representing a fighter belonging to the 244th Sentai. This is the "Tony" retained originally at Yokota AB by Occupation Forces

*(Kamikaze Museum)*

(34) Occupants of Ohka 11 kamikaze aircraft like this one, did not return. Symbolically, at Johnson AB (now Iruma AB), departing prominent USAF members and families of the base were given a "Sayonara" send-off with their names painted on this "Baka Bomb". It was returned to Japanese ownership in November 1963 and now resides in the base museum.

(44) Also resting in the War Museum in Kyoto is this Nakajima Ki-84 "Frank". Evaluated by TAIU at Clark AB in the Philippines as S-17, it was once owned and flown by the Planes of Fame Museum in California.

(36) This salt water-consumed Mitsubishi A6M7 "Zeke", which is beyond restoration, makes a fascinating exhibit at the Kamikaze Museum, Chiran, Kagoshima Prefecture, Kyushu. *(Kamikaze Museum)*

(39) Mitsubishi A6M5 "Zeke" seen here when its restoration was completed in August 1991, belongs to Nobuo Harada, Tokyo. It was formally shown within the Aircraft Section of the Kawaguchiko Motor Museum. *(N Harada)*

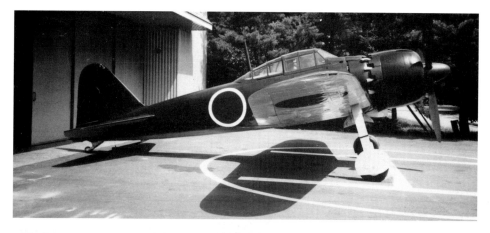

(41) Only the aft section was salvaged of this Mitsubishi G4M2 "Betty". It is now in restored condition and belongs to Nobuo Harada, Ohta, Tokyo. *(N Harada)*

(43) Another well restored Zero is this A6M5c. It resides in the War Museum in Kyoto, Japan.

零戦 Zero Fighter

(46) This Kawanishi H8K2 "Emily", was once with the 802 Kokutai, and captured by Occupation Forces intact on Shikoku, Japan. It was evaluated by the United States Navy at Patuxent River, Maryland in 1946/47, then stored for many years for the National Air and Space Museum. In 1979, it was returned to Japan. It is now exhibited at the Museum of Maritime Science, Tokyo.

(51) This Mitsubishi A6M5a Zero was restored by Mitsubishi Heavy Industries. It was recovered from Yap Island in 1984, and now resides at the Nagoya plant of Mitsubishi as a token of their earlier and very successful products.

*(T Kanamura)*

(48) Recovered from Yap Island, in the Carolines, this Yokosuka D4Y1 "Judy" was extensively restored at Kisarazu AB in 1980 where it is shown here. The restoration consists of a mix of D4Y2 parts with this basic D4Y1 airframe. The aircraft now resides at the Yasukuni Shrine, Tokyo. Tail code is of the 523rd Kokutai.

*(S Tanaka)*

(49) In the Yasukuni Shrine's Exhibition House in Tokyo is this well-represented reproduction of an Ohka II. This shrine is dedicated to the memories of the war dead which are enshrined here and has considerable public visitation.

(60) Beyond restoration, the exhibit of this Aichi D3A2 "Val" is being prepared at the Admiral Nimitz Center, Fredericksburg, Texas, as it might have been found in a jungle setting. This is an impressive method of preserving these remains in an unaltered state nearly as it was when found at Gasmata, New Britain Island.

*(Adm Nimitz Museum)*

(59) This Tachikawa Ki-36 Direct Co-operation Aircraft, code named "Ida", resides at the Royal Thai Air Force Museum, Bangkok. In service, this aircraft may have been used by the Thais as an advanced trainer because of its typical yellow-orange colour used for some training aircraft.

*(G Williams)*

(62) The US Air Force Museum in Dayton, Ohio, USA, retains this Kawanishi N1K2-J "George", now on indoor exhibit. It is one of three survivors of this type.

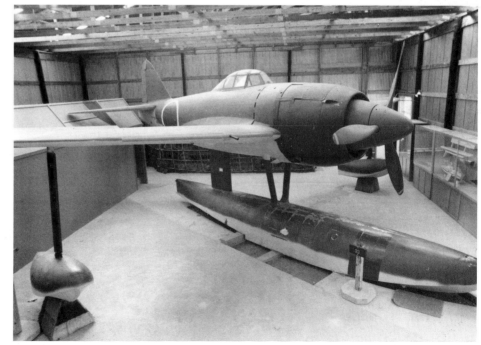

(61) This is one of four Kawanishi N1K1 "Rex" seaplane fighters taken to the US after the war. Stored for many years at Norfolk NAS, and still owned by the US Navy, it has been restored and is in an exhibit being prepared at the Admiral Nimitz Center, Texas.

*(Adm Nimitz Center)*

(66) One of two flying Zeros, this A6M2 of the Confederate Air Force, in Texas, US, is sponsored by Dr J L Kelley, and crewed by Norm Hartman. This Zero, now powered by a P & W R-1830-94 engine, was recovered by Bob Diemert from the island of Ballale, off Bougainville of the Solomons in the late 1970s. Quite probably, this aircraft was involved in the battle of the Coral Sea and the "Marianas Turkey Shoot". It carries early markings showing assignment to the aircraft carrier *Zuikaku*.
*(Bill Crump)*

(65) After many years outdoors as shown here at the Atlanta Museum, this Mitsubishi A6M5 "Zeke" now belongs to R D Wittington, Ft Lauderdale, Florida for restoration. It was assigned to the 261st Kokutai when captured on Saipan. The words "Technical Air Intelligence Center" can scarcely be seen from earlier paint under the cockpit. *(J Lansdale via J Long)*

(67) This Nakajima Ki-43-IIb "Oscar" of the National Air and Space Museum is on loan to the EAA Museum in Oshkosh, Wisconsin. It has the markings of the 248th Hiko Sentai (Flying Regiment) which operated in New Guinea, 1944.

(74) The restoration was begun in June 1989 on the Aichi M6A1 Seiran at the Smithsonian's National Air and Space Museum. This was a twin-float submarine-carried bomber of which six were preparing to bomb the Panama Canal shortly before the war ended. Fuselage seats behind the two floats.

(69) Battered but recognizable, this jungle recovered Kawasaki Ki-61 "Tony" resides in waiting for restoration at the Museum of Flying, Santa Monica, California.

(70) As with all Zeros exposed in humid climates for many years, this A6M3 Model 22 recovered from an Island off Indonesia in early 1991 will need new wing spars for this restoration project now underway at the Museum of Flying in California.

(71) This Mitsubishi G4M1 "Betty" was a major recovery operation from the South-west Pacific. The Museum of Flying is hopeful of its restoration with consideration given to flying status. Note early model gun blisters.

(72)  This Kugisho D4Y1 is an early model of "Judy" having the in-line liquid-cooled Atsuta 12 engine. This Japanese Navy dive bomber resides in the Museum of Flying in Santa Monica, California.

(76)  Residing for many years at NAS Willow Grove, Pennsylvania, this Kawanishi N1K2-J "George" now belongs to the NASM collection. Its restoration began in December 1991 at the Champlin Fighter Museum, Arizona. *(NASM 83-8082-38)*

(79) One of two NASM restored Japanese aircraft is this Zero Fighter which hangs in the World War II Gallery in Washington, DC. This A6M5 was captured on Saipan in June 1944 and test-flown in the US before the war ended.

(83) The Nakajima J1N1 "Irving" that belongs to the National Air and Space Museum, has been restored for preservation purposes. It, like many other aircraft, awaits an NASM building in which it can be on public display.

(85) The Nakajima Ki-115 Tsurugi was photographed here in 1991 when it was temporarily assembled for a TV documentary. This kamikaze aircraft is part of the National Air and Space Museum's collection. Its all sheet steel fuselage shows age and rust.

(84) The unrestored Nakajima Kikka of the National Air and Space Museum has been seen for many years in this improper configuration. Correct jet engines attached to the wings would be much larger than implied here. Operationally, it would have been comparable with the Messerschmitt Me 262.

*(Smithsonian Institution)*

(89) The National Museum of Naval Aviation at Pensacola, Florida added this Mitsubishi A6M2 to its collection in 1991. Before major rebuilding recently, this Zero recovered by Bob Diemert of Canada had been exhibited at Quantico, Virginia and Liberal, Kansas. It now carries the tail code showing assignment to the *Zuikaku* aircraft carrier at the time of the Pearl Harbor raid.

*(Natl Museum of Naval Aviation)*

(90) This MXY7-K1 is a trainer version of the Ohka "Baka Bomb". It is exhibited at the Naval Memorial Museum in Washington, DC, in its original orange colour.

(93) One of about 14 "Baka Bombs" that survive is at the Planes of Fame Museum in California. This one rests on a transport dolly beside a Zero at the same museum.

*(Planes of Fame)*

(98)  This Mitsubishi A6M7 Zero belonging to the National Air and Space Museum, Washington, DC, was for many years on outdoor exhibit at Willow Grove NAS, Pennsylvania. It has been restored by, and on exhibit at, the San Diego Aerospace Museum in what is believed to be its original markings of the Yokosuka Kokutai.

(100)  This Mitsubishi J8M1 Shusui at the Planes of Fame Museum, Chino, California is a Japanese version of the German Messerschmitt Me 163B. The museum staff claims that this is an MXY8 test version of the J8M1 with wing and fuselage from separate aircraft. *(W Swisher)*

# BIBLIOGRAPHY

Aireview. *The Fifty Years of Japanese Aviation 1910 - 1960.* Book Two. Tokyo: Kantosha Col, Ltd., 1961.

Bueschel, Richard M. *Communist Chinese Air Power.* New York: Frederick A. Praeger, Publishers, 1968.

Bueschel, Richard M. "Forgotten Air Forces." *Royal Air Force Flying Review.* November 1957.

Dupuy, Trevor Nevitt. The Military History of World War II: Volume 13. The Air War in the Pacific: *Air Power Leads the Way.* New York: Franklin Watts, Inc., 1964

Dupuy, Trevor Nevitt. The Military History of World War II: Volume 14. *The Air War In the Pacific: Victory in the Air.* New York: Franklin Watts, Inc., 1964.

Ehrengardt, C J. "Japanese Fighters of the Armee de l'Air." Aero Album, Winter 1970.

Flintham, Victor. *Air Wars and Aircraft.* London: Arms and Armour, 1989.

Gallagher, James P. *Meatballs and Dead Birds.* Perry Hill, MD, Jon-Jay Publishers, 1972.

MacArthur, Reports of General MacArthur. *The Campaigns of MacArthur in the Pacific,* Volume I. Washington: GPO, 1966.

MacArthur. *MacArthur in Japan: The Occupation: Military Phase,* Volume I Supplement. Washington: GPO, 1966.

MacArthur. *Japanese Operations in the South-west Pacific Area,* Volume II—Part II. Washington: GPO, 1966.

Mikesh, Robert C. "What Happened to those Japanese Planes?" *American Aviation Historical Society Journal.* Spring 1973.

Mikesh, Robert C. "More About Those Japanese Planes." *American Aviation Historical Society Journal.* Winter 1978.

Mikesh, Robert C. "Made In Japan, Tested In America." *Airpower.* Part II. July 1982.

Mikesh, Robert C. "More Fuel For The Furnace Kings." (Post-War destruction of Japanese Aircraft.) *Air Classics.* October 1970.

Ogden, Bob. *Aircraft Museums and Collections of the World, 1: Asia,* Woodley, England: Bob Ogden, 1991.

United States Strategic Bombing Survey. *Japanese Air Power.* Washington: GPO, July 1946.

United States Strategic Bombing Survey. *Japan's Struggle to End the War.* Washington: GPO, 1 July 1946.

# INDEX